Praise for *Managing to Make a Difference*

"Larry Sternberg has delivered several training programs for AMC managers over the years, and he has truly made a positive difference in our company. I am pleased he has written *Managing to Make a Difference* because I know he helps managers grow."

—**Jeff Portman**, President and Chief Operating Officer, AMC, Inc.

"Around the year 2000, I worked with Larry Sternberg to develop a management training program for Marietta Memorial Hospital. Like *Managing to Make a Difference*, the program went beyond theory, emphasizing implementation in the workplace. That program played a key role in helping our managers improve their effectiveness. What Larry teaches works."

—**J. Scott Cantley**, President and CEO,
Marietta Memorial Hospital & Memorial Health System

"I have had the pleasure of working with Larry Sternberg twice in my career, at two different companies. He's the real deal—a transformational mentor who unfailingly follows the suggestions in his book and manages teams that consider their experiences with him to be extraordinary. After having the good fortune of joining him on the executive team at The Ritz-Carlton, Tysons Corner, I modeled my leadership style after his and truly believe his guidance has positively impacted thousands of employees. If you strive to become an effective, compassionate manager—one who truly makes a difference—this is a book you won't be able to put down."

—**Marie Minarich**, Director of Human Resources,
The Jefferson Hotel, Washington, DC

MANAGING
TO
MAKE
A
DIFFERENCE

MANAGING
TO
MAKE
A
DIFFERENCE

HOW TO

ENGAGE, RETAIN, AND DEVELOP TALENT

FOR

MAXIMUM PERFORMANCE

LARRY STERNBERG
KIM TURNAGE

WILEY

CONTENTS

SECTION VI Embrace Change   239

SECTION VII Invest in Your Own Growth   261

PREFACE

It is entirely possible to accomplish business goals and earn promotions without making a positive difference in your employees' lives. We wrote this book for managers who do want to make that kind a difference, as it adds a powerful source of meaning and satisfaction to their work lives. In fact, when managers intentionally focus on making a positive difference, it becomes easier (and more fulfilling) for them to achieve business goals and progress in their careers.

We want this book to serve as a guide to help you grow as a manager. Not only do we provide a series of lessons, we also suggest a set of practical "experiments" that enable you to put the principles into action and learn from your own experience.

Not only are our recommendations supported by research, but over the course of his career, Larry Sternberg has put into practice every recommendation in the book. These recommendations work in the real world.

More than one reader pointed out that the strategies and tactics we teach can be used with family and friends to make a big difference in their lives. We invite you to keep this in mind as you progress through the book.

ACKNOWLEDGMENTS

L arry wishes to thank the following people for their contributions to this book:

My wife, Salli, whose unconditional love, belief, and support lift me up in everything I do.

My coauthor, Kim Turnage, who improved the final product far beyond what it would have been without her. Kim, I love working with you.

My boss, Kimberly Rath, for her unequivocal and generous support of this book, without which it would not have happened at all.

Carolyn Weese, for her proofing, formatting, and many other important contributions in getting this work submitted to our publisher.

Raschelle Casebier, for her contributions in getting this work submitted.

Sigi Brauer and Horst Schulze, for teaching me and giving me opportunities to grow as a manager and leader.

Vicki Denfield, Steven Freund, Jim Horsman, Marie Minarich, Fadi Ramadan, and Eric Swanson—the executives at The Ritz-Carlton, Tysons Corner, who taught me and supported me in my leadership journey. Each of you has made a big difference in my life.

Keith McLeod and Steve Marx, whose early critique helped us make major improvements to the book.

Doug Rath, whose teaching and support over the years has helped me grow.

Kim wishes to thank and acknowledge:

Larry Sternberg, for trusting me to help make his dream of this book a reality. Larry, I love working with you, too. What's next?

My husband and best friend, Rick Turnage, who has kept the promise he made 26 years ago to grow with me and help me grow, and who also happens to be one of the very best managers I know.

My dad, Wayne Guthrie, who was my first example of a manager who makes a difference and whose positive influence lives on in the hearts and minds of all those he left behind.

My first and most constant teachers and mentors, my mother, Chris Guthrie, and my grandmother, Verlene Schoen.

All the teachers, coaches, mentors, and managers who invested in me and helped me grow, most especially Larry Meyer, Greg Olson, Doug Rath, Ray Myers, Gwyn Bagot, Nan Fullinwider, Gary Pepin, and my teacher, mentor, and friend of 27 years and counting, Calvin P. Garbin.

My children, Connor, Arin, and Peyton—individually and together, you have been my greatest teachers about the power of discovering and nurturing the strengths and talents that make each person unique.

INTRODUCTION

What is managing to make a difference? Ask the next five people you see to tell you about a manager who made a difference in their lives, and see what you hear. Here are some responses we got when we asked that question:

> "She was supportive and highly in tune with my strengths. She consistently looked for ways to maximize my potential, always recognized my work, and helped me realize how much value I added to the organization. She was a mentor and coach but, most importantly, a friend."
>
> — *Jess Karo describing her manager,*
> *Trisha Berry*

> "I had a manager on the police department who would inspire us before the DWI detail we had every year during the month of December. He would plan a theme for the month. His squad was called the South West Weasels. The first year was 'Weasels in Wonderland.' He brought New Year's confetti poppers and sparkling grape juice to our kickoff. We drank to our success and sang songs. (Think of that—45 macho cops singing together!) He would then carefully assign people to various job tasks. The traffic oriented cops went out to stop cars. The more warm and fuzzy cops took calls for service. The burly ones were assigned to break up wild parties. Everyone was assigned to the jobs they were most successful at and gravitated toward. Job satisfaction was very high, and he played to people's strengths. Plus, everyone knew Mike had our back. No other brass would mess with Mike's squad. He was supportive, empathetic, the most creative person I have ever met, and he was all about our success and development. Additionally, he was a great resource and one of the best police officers I had ever seen. When I got promoted to Sergeant he mentored me. The first thing he told me was, 'Always come down on the side of your cops. No one else will stick up for them so you have to. They always get the benefit of the doubt.' Words cannot convey how formative he was for me."
>
> — *Kent Woodhead describing his manager,*
> *Mike Siefkes*

"I would thank her for being a positive moving force in my life. Our days would get very busy, and she worked alongside us to ensure we all met the goal together as one team. My manager was appreciative, supportive, gracious, and a dear friend. We don't work together anymore and I wish we did. Still friends today, she continues to shape my life and future for good."

—*Makenzie Rath describing her manager,*
Renuka Ramanathan

"He had two main gifts: seeing gifts in people that they didn't even know were there (and encouraging them to use those gifts!), and having a clear vision and goals, but at the same time making everyone around him feel like they were an important part of it all."

—*Matt Schur describing his manager,*
Larry Meyer

Try it yourself. This book is full of experiments, so make this your first one. Seriously. Ask the next five people you see to tell you about a manager who made a difference in their lives. They will not tell you about the business goals those managers achieved or the processes they improved or the awards they won. They will tell you about how those managers saw something in them, fanned a spark into a flame, and helped them grow. They will use words like trust, mentor, coach, grow, inspire, listen, empathy, potential—and friend. Those are the managers who make a difference—the ones who make people their highest priority and, as a bonus for that investment, achieve more, and perform better.

We wrote this book for managers who want to make a positive difference in the lives of the people they lead. We designed it as a kind of handbook. Each chapter stands alone so you can, if you like, open the book at random and start anywhere. But we also put the chapters in an order that allows them to build on one another as the book progresses. In this book, we provide real-life stories along with a series of lessons. We also suggest a set of practical "experiments" that enable you to put the principles into action and learn from your own experience.

Not only are the recommendations in this book supported by research, but over the course of his career, Larry Sternberg has put every single one into practice in his own work as a manager and leader. These recommendations work in the real world, and our experience tells us that, as you strive to be the kind of manager who makes a difference, you will not only improve engagement, performance, and retention among your team members (which translates to better results for your organization), you will also find a greater sense of fulfillment and meaning in your own work.

As you incorporate the lessons and experiments in this book into your daily work as a manager, you will increase your capacity to make a difference in the lives of the people you manage. The strategies you learn in this book can also carry over into your interactions with family and friends so that you make a bigger difference in their lives, too. And if someone asks a person you have managed, "Tell me about a manager who made a difference in your life," the manager he or she describes could very well be you.

CULTIVATE POSITIVE RELATIONSHIPS

Chapter 1

RELATIONSHIPS CREATE OPPORTUNITIES TO MAKE A DIFFERENCE

S ometimes moments of enlightenment are not about matters of profound wisdom. But they are moments of enlightenment, nevertheless.

Bernie Goes on a Bender

In the early 1980s, in Atlanta, Georgia, I experienced an important moment of enlightenment about turnover and retention of employees.

I love diners and it is my custom to have breakfast on my way to work. I always eat at the same diner. Over time, I get to know many of the employees, and they get to know me. So it was in Atlanta, during the time I was corporate director of human resources for a prominent hotel company.

One morning, as I walked through the door, Shirley poured my coffee and put in my order. She did not need to ask me; I always had two eggs over easy, with grits, toast, and bacon, crisp. As I took my seat at the counter, I noticed that one of the cooks was not there and had not been working for a few days. So I asked Shirley, "Is Bernie okay?" She replied that he had been absent and had not called in. It was evident that she was worried.

A couple of days later Bernie was back on the line cooking my breakfast. Naturally, I asked what happened. Bernie had gone on a drinking binge (my father would have called it a "bender") and had finally surfaced in a small

(continued)

(*continued*)

town many miles away. Someone from the diner had gone there to bring him home. The other employees were very angry with him. In fact, Shirley was not speaking to him.

This was my dramatic moment of enlightenment. Bernie had simply come back to work. Albeit with the need to atone for his transgression, but he had returned to work.

I realized that, in my company, Bernie would have been terminated for "three days no show no call," because we had a highly sophisticated set of rules and policies that had to be administered consistently. Consequently, we would not have been able to make an exception for Bernie.

Did I mention that Bernie had 17 years' tenure at this diner? Shirley, who was the low seniority employee, had been there for only 10 years.

This diner, which could not have been more "Mom and Pop," was out-performing me on the issue of retention. In part, it was because they did not have an employee handbook with a set of policies that required Bernie to be terminated. As I began to reflect on this issue, I realized that the purpose of many of our rules was to make it easy to fire people.

Think about employee orientation and employee handbooks. In many companies, the theme seems to be, "Welcome to our company! We want to make sure you know the reasons you can be punished (up to and including termination!)."

We make everyone sign a document (usually the last page of the handbook) attesting that they have read these rules. We need the signature, of course, in case we have to prove in court that they were aware of the rules and of the consequences of not abiding by them. We start building our case for termination on their first day of work!

You can probably cite numerous reasons why this is a good idea in today's litigious business environment. Maybe you believe such rules are a good business strategy. Maybe you are a little more ambivalent and would prefer not to have these kinds of rules, but you consider them a necessary evil. Either way, be honest about whether or not they contribute positively to retention. They do not.

In business, we often invest more in ensuring that we can fire our poor performers than we do in retaining our good performers. Rules designed to make it easy to fire people also make it more difficult to retain them.

All human communities have rules and need rules to function effectively. Even that diner had unwritten rules, and Bernie violated one when he did not call to tell his coworkers what was going on. But his punishment was that people were angry. Just like a family. Many organizations say that they are "like a family." The diner was actually living it.

Why was the diner able to function without a set of written rules? Relationship.

At the diner, people resolved their challenges through relationship rather than rules. That's what this book is about:

THE POWER AND IMPORTANCE OF RELATIONSHIPS

The late Dr. William E. Hall taught psychology at the University of Nebraska–Lincoln and studied relationships for more than 50 years. He was a pioneer in the field of positive psychology. Dr. Hall defined *relationship* in this way: "Relationship is the response one human being makes to another human being." This might strike you as oversimplified. It struck me that way when I first heard it. But over the past 25 years, I have come to appreciate its wisdom. Just think about it for a minute. If I respond to you in ways that you view as helpful or supportive in some way, you characterize our relationship as positive. If I respond to you in ways that you consider unhelpful, unsupportive, or hurtful, you characterize our relationship as negative. If I do not respond to you, we do not have a relationship.

If you are a manager, the relationships you cultivate with people have tremendous power. This book will help you cultivate the kinds of relationships that make a difference. People spend the majority of their waking hours at work. How can you cultivate the kinds of relationships that get people excited about coming to work, win their loyalty to your leadership, and cement their commitment to your organization? Building those kinds of relationships matters, not just because people matter but also because those kinds of relationships drive the growth and profitability of organizations. Here are some eye-opening research findings about how managers make a difference:

1. Managers do the coaching that hones potential into top performance. Top performers are 19 to 48 percent more productive than others, depending on the type of job.[1]
2. Managers influence at least 75 percent of the reasons people give for voluntary job turnover.[2]
3. The impact managers have on engagement and turnover goes straight to the bottom line. Disengaged employees cost organizations $3,400 for every $10,000 in salary, and turnover costs range from 48 to 61 percent of an employee's annual salary.[3]

In this book we provide a lot of concrete suggestions for managing to make a difference—so many suggestions that we do not expect anybody to try them all. Our purpose is to help you identify approaches that suit your unique style. Think of your part of the organization as your laboratory. You are in the laboratory every day. You can experiment with different tools and tactics. Just pick something that appeals to you and try it. And then pay attention to your results. If it works for you, keep doing it. If it does not work, quit doing it.

The suggestions we offer come from over 50 years of combined leadership and consulting experience focused on best practices in engaging, retaining, and developing top performers. We have partnered with individuals and organizations to create great places to work in which people grow and relationships thrive. We do not claim that our approach is the only way, but it is effective, positive, and affirming. It is the furthest thing from motivational fluff. It is reality-based in every way.

The successful use of these best practices involves accepting the following realities:

1. Relationships in the workplace matter. In particular, the relationship between an employee and his or her manager has the biggest impact on that person's engagement, retention, and development. Therefore, as a manager, you can make a huge difference.
2. Adults have identifiable patterns of thoughts, feelings, and behavior that are deeply ingrained and very difficult to change. We will call these patterns "themes."
3. Aptitude exists. Aptitude is the natural *potential* to do certain things really well—possibly at a very high level of excellence. In discussing aptitude, we will often use the words *talent* and *giftedness*.
4. Every person has aces and spaces—things they naturally do well and things they naturally just do not do well.

One more thing before you dig in. It is important to recognize that the results you are getting now are based on the ways you are doing things now. If you want the same results going forward, do things the same way. If you want significantly improved results, you have to have the courage to ask, "What can I do differently?" We recognize that there are real risks involved in trying new methods. That is why it takes courage. But it is the only way to improve. If you have the courage to experiment, we offer some great places to start.

Chapter 2

GET TO KNOW YOUR EMPLOYEES

The first step in cultivating positive relationships is getting to know your people. Right away, we are giving you a simple, practical tool that will help you rapidly build positive relationships with people you have just met. It will also help you improve relationships with people you already know. The tool, called "Focus On You®," consists of the following six questions.

FOCUS ON YOU

1. What name do you prefer to be called?
2. If you boil it all down to a few words, what do you really get paid to do?
3. What are your positive hot buttons—your interests in and out of work that are instant conversation starters?
4. Tell us about two successes you have had, one professional and one personal.
5. What do you do best—in and out of work?
6. Tell us about two goals you have, one professional and one personal.

To use this tool with one or more people, hand out a blank copy of the Focus On You Worksheet to everyone and explain the six questions. Give everyone (including yourself) a few minutes to make notes on their own responses to the six questions in the boxes provided. Take turns allowing each person (including yourself) to share their answers to all the questions, without interruption. Then invite follow-up questions. Each person should take three to five minutes. Take notes on what everyone says. These notes are worth keeping and referring back to

Name	What Do I Get Paid to Do?	Hot Buttons	Successes: 1 Professional 1 Personal	What I Do Best	Goals: 1 Professional 1 Personal
Kim	help leaders grow their people & organizations	Rick · Connor Ann · Payton track & field leadership books	being a trusted advisor to my clients ------- 36 yr marriage & 3 amazing young adults	ask write think coach care deliver	finish this book ! ------- help my kids grow into their unique strengths
Larry	Help people & organizations grow	Salli (wife) creativity Talent+ public speaking humor bourbon	developing numerous leaders ------- marriage	think teach facilitate lead	achieve 20% revenue growth ------- consistent health habits
			-------		-------
			-------		-------
			-------		-------

Talent+.

Figure 2.1

later. We have provided an example that includes Kim's notes on her own answers and her notes on Larry's answers to the six questions. You can find printable Focus On You worksheets on our website at ManageToMakeADifference.com.

Focus On You works one-on-one or in groups. You must do this in person, face to face, and you must always answer the questions yourself. The point of Focus On You is for everyone involved to learn a few things about everyone else.

EXPERIMENT: CONDUCT FOCUS ON YOU

1. Conduct Focus On You with your current direct reports. Take notes on what they say.
2. Highlight in your notes everything new you learned about each person.
3. Conduct Focus On You with every new hire on your team within their first two days on the job. Remember that you must answer the questions, too.
4. After you have completed steps 1 through 3, answer this question: How has this made a difference?

Note: You can also do Focus On You with significant others or friends. Hal, a seminar participant and senior vice president for a large manufacturing company, did Focus On You with his family. He found out he was calling his daughter, Melissa, by the wrong name. She preferred Missy. Focus On You was only a small portion of the seminar he attended, but Hal insisted that outcome with his daughter, on its own, was worth every penny he paid for the seminar.

GO AHEAD, GET CLOSE TO YOUR PEOPLE

M any managers are taught, "Do not get too close to your people. Be friendly with them, sure. But you need to know where to draw the line." Sound familiar? Unfortunately, practicing this approach diminishes your ability to motivate and retain your top performers. Again, you have to choose your basic philosophy. Do you want to conduct your relationships so that it is easier to fire people or do you want to respond to people in ways that enhance retention?

What level of relationship should you have with your coworkers? Where should you draw the line? Our answer is: *Do not place limits on the depth of your friendships with coworkers.* The world is full of misguided thinking that passes for wisdom. People are taught not to get close with their coworkers or with their direct reports. Do not heed that advice.

Think about the reasons that people tell you not to get too close.

"Familiarity breeds contempt," is one of the most commonly repeated reasons.

If that statement were true, the people who have the most contempt for you would be your closest friends and relatives!

Here is the next reason people advocate not getting too close to your employees:

"You may have to discipline that person."

The fact that it is emotionally unpleasant to discipline someone you are close to is a *good* thing. You will first try to persuade them through conversation that they will be better off if they change their behavior. The closer your relationship, the

11

more likely you can influence them to correct their behavior before you need to resort to disciplinary action. And if you do need to go there, these employees will see that it is painful for you. And that sends the right message.

LESSON

The closer your relationship is with someone, the easier it is to influence that person to change his or her behavior.

"But," some will say, "if you are too close to that employee, you might avoid the discipline because you don't want to hurt their feelings or damage your relationship."

That is a powerful point. Many managers fall into the trap of avoiding close relationships for exactly that reason. They do not reflect on the fact that it is your closest friends, the people who care most about you, who are willing to deliver difficult messages. Who tells you that you have bad breath? Not a stranger, usually. Why is that? Because the person who tells you knows that the interaction will be uncomfortable at best, and it might hurt your feelings. But someone who cares about you is willing to work through those uncomfortable feelings to help you. The stranger does not need the hassle.

If you are a parent, think about the times you have delivered difficult messages to your children—messages that possibly made them cry. Why did you do that? Because you enjoy hurting their feelings? Of course not. You did it because you wanted to help them be the best person they could be and you knew that they needed to hear what you had to say. You care so much about them that you are willing to work through the hurt feelings.

LESSON

The closer you are to someone and the more you care about them, the more willing you are to have difficult and unpleasant conversations. The other person will know that you have their best interests at heart.

Great managers do not let their relationships prevent them from doing their jobs, even when they must discipline their friends.

The Concierge

This is a story about Horst Schulze, legendary chief operating officer of The Ritz-Carlton Hotel Company. At one point, Horst was the general manager of a hotel that was hosting a major dog show. Dogs are not known for their discretion about where they poop. So he hired a number of temps whose job was to walk around the public spaces and scoop the poop.

He noticed one young man, Walt, who had a terrific personality. In addition to scooping the poop, Walt was smiling and cheerfully greeting passersby—just what you want hotel employees to do. Furthermore, he had taken the initiative to learn the names of the meeting rooms so that he could help people with directions.

After the temp job was over, Horst gave Walt a job and became his mentor. Over the years, Walt became an excellent hospitality professional, and they became friends as well. Wherever Horst went, Walt followed, steadily advancing in his career.

One day, the hotel security department caught Walt doing an illegal activity while on the job. Termination was the only option. Horst was devastated. He literally cried, but he did his job.

The employees in the hotel knew the facts. And they saw that Horst did not try to make an exception or cover up the incident to save his friend's job. People respected that.

LESSON

People do not lose respect for you because you become friends with some employees. They lose respect when you decide not to do your job as a manager.

Look at the next objection to forming close relationships:

"People will accuse me of having favorites."

Here is reality: *You have favorites now.*

It is human nature. You have better chemistry with some employees than with others. And, by the way, your employees know very well who your favorites are. You might not treat these people differently in terms of rewards, shift preferences, rule enforcement, et cetera. But people know that you have favorites. So . . .

LESSON

Don't worry about having favorites because it is unavoidable. Just make sure that you give people rewards based on performance, not based on the relationship.

"But," you may ask, "what are the benefits of forming close relationships with my employees? It is fraught with risk. Why should I take these risks?"

Imagine you have a very serious problem in your life, a problem in which you need someone to show up on your doorstep tomorrow morning. The deadline is nonnegotiable. They must show up tomorrow morning. Who would you call? Who would absolutely do this for you? Have a real person in mind before you read further.

You are probably thinking of someone with whom you have a close relationship. Your certainty that this person will show up to help is based *entirely on your relationship.*

Managers who are close to their people can ask for more effort and better results. They can ask people to hang in during difficult times. They can ask people to try a new process. They can ask for forgiveness when they have exercised poor judgment. And even when they do not ask, managers who are close to their people inspire more discretionary effort. Discretionary effort is people's willingness to go above and beyond, to do more than the minimum requirement.

LESSON

When you have close, positive relationships with your people, they will do things for you, not because there is some reward for them, but simply because they care about you . . . And because they know you care about them.

But doesn't this go both ways so that they can now ask you, their manager, for more effort and better results?

Yes, it does. If you are not willing to extend yourself for your people, why would they extend themselves for you?

LESSON

Your proactive efforts to strengthen the relationships with the people you manage will increase motivation, engagement, and loyalty.

Some readers will definitely be uncomfortable with this approach and will outright reject it for the reasons discussed in this chapter. That's okay. Every manager has his or her own style. Relationships—personal as well as professional—always involve risk.

But we know there are some managers out there who have questioned the common advice to keep a distance, to draw a line. We are speaking to you. In your heart of hearts, you have said to yourself, "Things feel better when I get close to my people." To you, we say: Go for it. Give it a try. See what results you get in your laboratory. The risks are well worth the rewards.

EXPERIMENT: STRENGTHEN RELATIONSHIPS

1. Find opportunities to get together with your employees outside of work. Do this at least every couple of weeks, or more often.
2. If you are inclined to pursue friendships with certain employees, do it.
3. Find out what is going on in people's personal lives. Demonstrate that they are of interest to you.
4. After 90 days, think about how this has made a difference. Are people more supportive of each other? Do you sense an improved esprit de corps? Has morale improved?

ACCEPT PEOPLE AS THEY ARE

A ccepting people as they are—not asking them to change—is the most important aspect of cultivating positive relationships. In fact, *this is the most important chapter in the book. This chapter can change your life.*

Bill's Lesson Learned

A friend, Bill Kerrey, tells this story. His daughter did not keep her room neat and tidy and Bill was determined to help her change that.

Every weekday he would drive her home from school. The drive was tense because they both knew that when they got home, he would look at her room right away. Every day it was messy, and every day the evening went downhill from there. He tried every technique in the book (and some that were not in the book) to motivate her to change. Nothing worked.

One day he realized that his focus on keeping her room neat was damaging their relationship, and he realized that his relationship with his daughter was way more important to him than a clean room.

That day on the drive home he asked her about her day. When they got home he did not inspect her room. He just closed the door. He figured out that if he did not see it, it would not bother him. So he just quit focusing on her room, and he quit asking her to change. He accepted her as she was.

Bill reports that his relationship with his daughter improved *overnight*.

Dr. William E. Hall defined a "life theme" as a pattern of thoughts, feelings, and behaviors that is persistent over time. Every time you describe someone, you are naming themes: cheerful, thoughtful, lazy, organized, courageous—get the picture? These descriptions help us predict the behaviors we are likely to observe in others.

If you want to understand just how persistent themes are, think about your most recent school reunion (or some similar event). Did not you see the same themes you saw when you knew those people years ago? The class clown is still the class clown. The gossips still gossip. The introverts are still quiet. Themes persist over time and are particularly resistant to change.

Despite the fact that people tend not to change, we are quite cavalier about asking people to change anyway. We do this all the time in performance evaluations and in 360 feedback. Do any of these examples sound familiar?

1. Do not be so sensitive.
2. You need to be more organized.
3. You need to be more detail oriented.
4. You do not demonstrate a sense of urgency.
5. You are late to meetings all the time. This has to change.
6. You need to be more assertive.
7. You are too much of a perfectionist.

We drastically underestimate how difficult it is to change these deeply ingrained patterns.

Marry As Is; If You Get a Change, It's a Bonus

A seminar participant once asked, "Do you mean my husband is never going to change?" In response to the question, "Can you tell me more?" she explained.

"I'm very goal oriented and my husband is very laid back—a go-with-the-flow kind of guy. Last Saturday, he left the house at 10:00 AM to run some errands. He had six things he was going to do. He returned home at 2:00 PM and he had done only two! So I said to him, 'What about the other four?' 'Don't worry,' he replied, 'I'll get them another time.' Do you mean to tell me that is never going to change?"

I asked, "Suppose it does not change? Would you still love him? Would you still want to remain married to him?"

"Of course," she replied, "but what can I do about this?"

"Get off his back! Quit asking him to change. Accept him as he is."

Everyone you know has people in their lives who are trying to help them improve. But they are doing it by focusing on eliminating flaws and remediating weaknesses. Everyone has plenty of help on that agenda. *You have the opportunity to be one of the few people who focus on what is right about a person rather than what is wrong.*

LESSON

Marry as is. If you get a change it is a bonus. When you quit asking people to change, you will change your relationships. And when you change your relationships you will change your life.

Of course this applies not only to your personal relationships, but also to your professional ones, and particularly to your relationships with the people you manage.

EXPERIMENT: QUIT ASKING PEOPLE TO CHANGE

1. Identify two people you are asking to change—one in your personal life and one in your professional life.
2. Just quit asking them to change. Accept them as they are.
3. Notice what happens to your relationship.

TOLERATE UNDESIRABLE BEHAVIORS

If you are committed to cultivating positive relationships with people through accepting them as they are, you will inevitably run into conflicts between how people really are and how you wish they would be. What will you do in those instances? Where will you draw the line when accepting people as they are rubs you the wrong way?

The General Manager and the Director of Sales

I was teaching a seminar for a group of hotel general managers and one of them said, "Larry, help me apply what you're talking about to my director of sales. She is notoriously late to all meetings. And we have a standard that if we say a meeting that starts at eight, we do not mean 8:05."

This was a luxury hotel in which timeliness was a sign of excellence, precision, and attention to detail. Meetings started on time. The general manager was asking, "Given our culture and standards, what am I supposed to do about this? We consider that behavior disrespectful toward the other people in the meeting."

I said, "Well, tell me about the director of sales. How is she doing against the budgeted goals?"

He replied, "She's blowin' 'em away."

"Okay," I said, "how is she doing with her people? Is she a good mentor?"

(continued)

21

(*continued*)

"Oh yeah," he said, "she trains people, and we promote them out to other hotels. People are standing in line to get into this department to work for her."

I responded, "What's your problem?"

"She's late to meetings!"

I said, "Do you want a director of marketing who is on time to meetings, or do you want a director of marketing who blows away her revenue goals and develops great people for your organization?"

He said, "I want it all!"

LESSON

With real human beings in the real world, you do not get it all. Everybody has aces and spaces. In both business and personal life, tolerance of shortcomings is required to cultivate close positive relationships.

In every job there are things that are Nice to Have (such as timeliness in the previous story) and Need to Have (such as the ability to close sales). Be most tolerant in the Nice-to-Have category.

But how much undesirable behavior should you tolerate? The unsatisfying answer is: it depends. The more valuable a person is to an organization, the more inclined an organization will be to give that person special treatment.

The Best Car Salesman

Hank, a general manager of a large, successful Lincoln-Mercury dealership told me this story. For context, it is important to understand that Saturday is an "all-hands-on-deck" day for car dealers. Nobody gets Saturday off.

Tom had been the number one salesman in this dealership for 18 years in a row. One day, he walked into Hank's office and said casually, "My son's playing football this year, so I'm taking Saturdays off to watch him play." This was not a request.

A seminar participant asked, "What did you do?" Without hesitation, Hank replied, "I gave him Saturdays off. He's my top guy."

EXPERIMENT: TOLERATING UNDESIRABLE BEHAVIORS

1. The next time one of your best people exhibits an annoying behavior, ask yourself, "Is that Nice to Have or Need to Have?" Be honest.
2. If it is Nice to Have, just let it go. Nobody is perfect. Accept him with all his aces and spaces.
3. Focus on helping that person amplify his talents and strengths—the things that really make a difference in his productive performance.
4. Do this with all of your direct reports for 90 days.
5. Reflect on what you have learned. Do you see a difference in morale and engagement? How do you feel now that you are not asking people to change things that do not really matter all that much?

The downside of this accommodation typically involves dissatisfaction from other employees. "Hey, why does *he* get Saturdays off?" Of course, this is an easy one. Hank can reply, "As soon as you're number one for 18 consecutive years, I'll be happy to give you Saturdays off!" The downside of *not* giving the top guy Saturdays off is that he goes to another dealership. We are talking about favoritism here, but favoritism that is earned based on superior performance.

The Chef with Long Hair

I was on the pre-opening training team for The Ritz-Carlton Barcelona. My responsibilities included training the public space cleaning team. I do not speak Spanish so a couple of employees served as interpreters. We were enjoying lunch as a team in the employee dining room when Gunter came in to get a cup of coffee. Gunter was, at that time, the number one chef de cuisine in the entire company. Gunter had hair down to the small of his back, in flagrant violation of the company standard for male hair length.

All the employees on my team started speaking at once. I could see they were talking about Gunter, but I could not understand what they were saying, so I asked one of my interpreters. She said, "They are saying he must be really, really good at his job."

LESSON

Employees are eminently capable of understanding why you are tolerating certain kinds of undesired behavior from top performers. And what's more, they accept it.

A more challenging situation occurs when the top performer is undermining the culture, mistreating people, or acting immorally or unethically. How much of *that* should you tolerate? It is up to you. The decisions you make in these situations define what the fundamental values system of your culture really is. Where you draw the line in any situation speaks powerfully about what you really value.

Chapter 6

MAKE PEOPLE SIGNIFICANT

Sawubona is an African Zulu greeting that means, "I see you." It goes far beyond the rote, "Hello," or, "How are you?" so many of us say every day. *Sawubona* says, "I see deeper than the surface. I see your personality. I see what makes you unique. I see you as a person with dignity, worthy of my respect."

Ngikhona is the traditional response to *sawubona*. It means, "I am here." In the Zulu culture, the call *"Sawubona"* says, "I see you. You are a person." And the response, *"Ngikhona,"* says, "Because you see me, I am here." There is a question underneath that greeting: If you do not see me, do I exist? Indeed, the Zulu proverb *"Umuntu ngumuntu ngabantu"* means, "A person is a person because of other people."

Although not often discussed, the longing for significance is a basic human desire. Everybody wants to know that they are significant—someone truly cares about them, their existence has meaning, they matter, and they are making a noticeable difference in the world. So as a manager, helping employees (each and every one) become more significant makes a big difference in their lives. If each person you manage knows that he or she is truly significant to you, you dramatically increase their engagement and the likelihood of retaining them.

So how do you demonstrate that a person is significant to you? Dr. Shalom Saar is a professor at the Massachusetts Institute of Technology and at Cheung Kong Graduate School of Business in Beijing. A renowned authority on leadership, Dr. Saar taught me that caring and time are key factors in making people significant. They are related. The more I care about you, the more likely I am going to give you my time.

Genuine caring is not merely some feeling you have. Unless that feeling results in action, it has little value to the other person. Genuine caring means extending yourself to meet that person's needs, to support them, and to help them succeed.

Demonstrate to employees that you are their ally, not their judge. Demonstrate that you are fiercely interested in helping them succeed in their jobs, *but* not merely because that will help you. If you truly care about a person, you will extend yourself to help them *simply because it benefits them*.

Expressing genuine interest in your employees is a powerful way to demonstrate how much you care about them. Focus On You can be a great place for you to start, but do not stop there. Human relationships grow organically. This kind of growth cannot be accomplished solely through programs or through the use of tools, no matter how good they are. It takes daily commitment and repeated interaction to cultivate the strongest relationships. This insight about daily interactions applies to any relationship. Think about marriage, for example. It is good to express your love and gratitude on special occasions, such as your anniversary. But how you treat your spouse every single day is much more expressive of your true feelings than how you respond on your anniversary. So as a manager, find out what each employee values in life, understand their aspirations, and show interest in what is going on in their personal lives. Dr. Hall, who defined relationship as the response one person makes to another, taught that you can never know enough about another person, provided that you want to know for the right reason, which is to benefit that person.

LESSON

In cultivating the close, positive relationships that make people significant, your authentic, spontaneous daily interactions matter most. And those interactions, accumulated over time, positively affect people's engagement, retention, and growth.

In addition to daily interactions, showing up for major life events powerfully conveys significance. If you are cultivating close, positive relationships, employees are more likely to invite you to attend their major life events. Showing up makes a huge difference. This is a really big deal. It shows people that you care about the things they care about. This is what friends and family do. Be there for these occasions. Visit employees in the hospital. Celebrate engagements, promotions, graduations, the completion of major work projects. Be there for funerals too. Witnessing the events that matter most to your people adds to their sense of significance. We have seen it in action. We work for a company in which the most senior leaders (president and board members) rearrange their schedules and go to great lengths to be present at these types of events. Going to that kind of effort makes a major statement about other people's significance to them.

LESSON

Being present for major life events powerfully conveys how significant that person is to you.

Remember, Dr. Saar emphasizes both caring and time as key factors that demonstrate how significant a person is in your life. Spending time with people, not just on special occasions but on a daily and weekly basis, makes them more significant. Make yourself easily accessible. Give people your time when they want it.

Think about your relationship with your own manager. How easy is it for you to see her? Does she fit you in only when it is convenient for her, or does she show a higher sense of urgency to meet with you? Whatever her typical response is, what message does it send about your importance to her? How does that make you feel?

Now imagine for a moment that your very best customer or the president of your company came to her workplace unexpectedly. No appointment. No advance notice. How would your boss respond then? Would she not rearrange her schedule to speak with that person right away?

We can see this in personal life as well. When you invite someone to spend some time with you, that person's response sends you a clear message about how much he or she really wants to spend time with you.

As a manager, what can you take away from all this?

LESSON

The more important someone is, the more likely you will meet with that person when he or she wants to meet, not merely when it is convenient for you. Your employees know that, by the way.

How easy is it for an employee to speak with you one-on-one? An open door is the best approach. Unless you are actively involved with a customer or another employee, meet with that employee in the moment, right when he comes to you. If you cannot meet with him when he wants, do you have a sense of urgency about getting together as soon as possible?

No matter how sincerely you believe that you have no space in your schedule to meet with him until next week, that person who wants time with you knows that, if he were important enough, you would meet with him as soon as possible. Whether you like it or not, you are sending a message.

When one of your employees wants to meet with you or speak with you, that person has a need at that moment. When you interrupt what you are doing to listen to that need, you are demonstrating that person's significance to you.

The Administrative Assistant

Almost 30 years ago, I accepted a position as corporate director of human resources for a prominent hotel company. During my initial introduction, the president and two of the vice presidents informed me that, regrettably, my administrative assistant needed to be fired because of a poor attitude. The person who preceded me in the job, they said, should have done that before he left.

As I got to know her, I soon realized that she had excellent skills and knowledge for her job. I noticed, however, that to be at her best, she needed at least 30 minutes of my time every day just to discuss what was going on in the company. She would not have been able to articulate that need, by the way. I had to discern it. The former director did not give her this time, and that was the root cause of the attitude problem.

I decided to give her the time she needed, and the attitude problems completely disappeared.

You may be thinking, "This principle about giving people time sounds good in theory, but I simply can't get my work done if I practice an open-door policy."

That might be true, but don't fool yourself. When you do not make time for people on their terms, you diminish the likelihood of retaining them because the message is clear: *I have more important things to do than to listen to you.* Conversely, when you make time on their terms, you have the potential to enjoy significant gains in their performance, productivity, and engagement.

When you do spend time with people, what you do makes a difference, too. One-on-one time with the people you manage is a time to forget about multitasking.

What Larry Learned from Darryl Hartley-Leonard

When I was with Hyatt Hotels, Darryl Hartley-Leonard was the executive vice president. He was a genius at making people feel significant. I did not meet with him often, but here's how it went when I did. I would sit across his desk and he would pick up the phone and ask his assistant, "Please hold my calls while I'm with Larry." He could have asked that earlier, but he wanted me to know it. He would then sweep things aside on his desk so that there were no objects or papers between us. And for the time we were together, he focused only on me. He did a lot of listening. He was not rushed to conclude the meeting so he could get to the next thing. He made me feel like the only person who mattered during that time.

When you meet with an employee, are you fully present? Are you really listening? Or do you check your computer or phone?

What you do with your phone sends a message about how important the person is. There is actually research on this topic. It shows that just having a phone visible on the table has a negative impact on your relationship with the other person. The mere presence of your cell phone diminishes closeness, trust, and the other person's sense that you are extending empathy and understanding in the interaction. That negative impact is most intense when individuals are discussing a personally meaningful topic (Przybylski and Weinstein).[1]

LESSON

Be fully present when meeting with your people. The more important a person is, the more likely you will turn off your phone while you are with him or her.

EXPERIMENT: MAKE PEOPLE FEEL SIGNIFICANT

1. Notice the kind of conversation you have with good friends. In particular, notice how you ask about their vacation, their weekend, their family, and so forth.
2. Make a point of having those kinds of conversations with your employees.
3. Practice an open-door policy as often as possible.
4. Celebrate milestones and major life events. Show up, even when it is inconvenient for you.
5. Turn off your phone when meeting with an employee. Go one step further and put it in a drawer or in your bag.
6. Do those things for 90 days. Reflect on how this behavior has made a difference. In particular, notice whether turning your phone off for a while caused you a problem.

Chapter 7

PRIORITIZE ONE-ON-ONES

This chapter begins with a simple but profound lesson:

LESSON
The most important and meaningful meetings are one-on-one.

You can verify this insight by thinking about your life experience. This is how mentoring works. This is how sales are closed. Think about the last conference you attended. Did you derive more value from the keynotes and breakouts or from one-on-one conversations with the people you met at the conference? Think about how things get done in your organization or in your life. In your experience, do you get better results and get them faster from one-on-one conversations or from group meetings?

We invite you to review how much one-on-one time you are investing with the people you manage. And most important, we invite you to review with whom you are investing this time. Are you investing enough one-on-one time with your direct reports? With top performers? With others who are important to the organization?

Unfortunately, most of us are too busy to rely on happenstance to present enough one-on-one opportunities. We have to be more intentional. We have to schedule them. Changing your routine in this way might require you to eliminate some activities to make time in your schedule for one-on-one meetings.

Here is the payoff, though. You powerfully demonstrate to the other person that he or she is significant to you, you enrich your relationship, you enhance engagement, you learn more about people's individual aspirations and needs, you move initiatives forward, and you achieve better alignment. What's not to like?

Here are some research-based answers to questions managers often ask about one-on-ones based, in part, on data collected by The Ken Blanchard Companies.[1]

HOW FREQUENTLY SHOULD YOU MEET?

You will hit the mark for the majority of people with monthly one-on-ones—89 percent of people want to meet with their manager at least once a month. But only 73 percent actually get a monthly one-on-one. Of course, you should be sensitive to individual differences—44 percent of people want to meet once a week or more (and only 34 percent of people actually do).

In thinking about the frequency, remember that some of these meetings will be canceled for a variety of very good reasons. Make sure you do not go more than 90 days without a one-on-one.

HOW LONG SHOULD THOSE MEETINGS LAST?

Most people (65 percent) just need 30 minutes to an hour. About 25 percent are happy with 30 minutes or less, and only 10 percent want more than an hour. Again, it is important to individualize. But nobody needs your whole day.

WHAT SHOULD YOU DISCUSS IN THESE MEETINGS . . . AND WHO SHOULD DECIDE?

The majority of people (69 percent) want to take responsibility for setting the agenda. For the remaining 31 percent, it is critical to ask the kinds of questions that ensure you meet their individual needs in a one-on-one session.

Here are some key takeaways on how people want to allocate time in one-on-one conversations with their managers:

- People want to spend a lot more time than they actually do in one-on-one conversations about goal setting, goal review, performance feedback, problem solving, and soliciting specific support. The bad news: *28 percent rarely or never have goal-setting conversations with their managers and 36 percent rarely or never have performance feedback conversations.* **Don't be that manager.**
- Only 5 percent of people want to discuss personal issues "often" or "all the time." We want to clarify that our interpretation of this is *not* that people do not want a personal connection with you. In the ideal relationship, conversations about life outside work happen spontaneously. But when you are in a scheduled one-on-one meeting, most of the people on your team

want to spend that valuable time with you discussing all the other issues that affect their performance, professional growth, and contribution to the success of the business. While it is critically important to be responsive and supportive when people reach out for support on personal issues, it is likely to remain rare in the context of business-focused one-on-ones.

The survey results discussed here reveal some trends, but there is absolutely no substitute for *asking* each person on your team what they need and want. *Remember: The Goldilocks Zone is going to be different for each person.*

EXPERIMENT: START ONE-ON-ONE MEETINGS

1. Ask these questions with the people you manage:
   - How often would you like to meet with me one-on-one?
   - How long would you like those meetings to last?
   - How should we set the agenda?
   - What topics of conversation are most important and urgent for you?
   - What topics of conversation are highly important but less urgent and how do we make sure we get to these topics at the right frequency?
2. Begin your one-on-ones. Do your best not to cancel or move them.
3. After 90 days, reflect on what you have learned. Did you discover information that would not have come to you otherwise? How did these meetings help you? How did they help your people?

As a manager, your time is precious. How can you prioritize one-on-ones without letting them blow up your schedule? Here are some suggestions:

- Proactively schedule one-on-ones and make them a "rock" in *both* people's schedules.
- When changes to scheduled one-on-ones must be made, reschedule immediately.
- Walk around, pop in to people's offices without an agenda, and have a real open-door policy (if your door is open, it is not an interruption for someone to come in).

If one-on-one meetings are new for you (and even if they are not), you might find the next experiment using the Career Investment Discussion (CID) to be a helpful resource in sparking the kind of productive discussion that only happens when you ask open-ended questions.

The CID is a specific type of one-on-one meeting. Conversations between leaders and direct reports are frequently about what the leader wants from that person or some comment on that person's performance. By contrast, a CID is a series of questions that enables managers to discover how they can improve their contributions to the success and growth of their direct reports. This kind of interaction also contributes enormously to a person's sense of significance.

EXPERIMENT: TRY QUARTERLY CAREER INVESTMENT DISCUSSIONS

1. Once a quarter, devote your one-on-one to a CID.
2. Ask the following questions in one-on-one meetings with each direct report.
3. Take good notes. You can find a printable version of the CID on our website at ManageToMakeADifference.com.
4. Do something about what you hear.
5. Review your notes from the last CID before you do the next one with that same person.
6. Note: The first couple of times you do this, people might find it challenging to answer, but they will get into it over time. For some people, it may be helpful to have the questions ahead of time so they can spend more time reflecting on their responses. Individualize based on what you know about people's themes.

   - Tell me about your recent successes and high points.
   - What goals are you working on right now?
   - How can I help?
   - Is there a strength you would like to use more of?
   - On a 1-to-10 scale, with 10 being high, to what degree is your potential being maximized?
   - (if less than 9) What can I do to help you move that number up?
   - What percentage of your time do you spend doing things you are good at and enjoy?
   - (if less than 90 percent) What can I do to help you move that number up?
   - What would you like to learn?
   - How are you growing?
   - Is there anything else you would like to discuss?

7. After two meetings, reflect on what you have learned. How have these meetings helped you? How have they helped your people?

Undoubtedly, you will think of additional questions that are valuable in your unique situation. Questions will be most effective when they are open ended and push people beyond yes-or-no responses.

There is a secret to getting the most out of a CID and it is also a lesson:

LESSON

Just asking the questions and listening are not enough. You must *act* on the information, and you must act as rapidly as you can.

Just like the Focus On You, the CID is not a magic bullet. It is a tool you can use to enhance the impact of the time you regularly invest in one-on-ones with the people on your team. But never use it as a standalone or as a substitute for doing the dailies. Remember, your daily interactions matter most. When, in the course of your daily interactions with people, you are consistently accepting them as they are, making them feel significant, and prioritizing one-on-one time with them, you will naturally increase their happiness, enhance their engagement, grow their loyalty to your leadership, and cement their commitment to your organization.

Chapter 8

DON'T MAKE RELATIONSHIP CONFLICTS WORSE

R elationship problems exist in every organization. Cultivating positive relationships with your people does not happen in a vacuum, and it does not make conflict go away completely (but it can reduce conflict because it proactively addresses some of its root causes). Research suggests that 64 percent of people wish they could talk about problems with colleagues "often" or "all the time" in one-on-one conversations with their managers. Fortunately, only about 8 percent actually do).[1] Don't get sucked into this. It perpetuates negativity and undermines positive relationships.

Quit Mediating Relationships

When I first became an HR director, I invested a huge amount of time mediating and refereeing relationships, and my fellow managers joined me. Employees would come into my office—every day—to complain about being treated poorly in any number of ways. These types of complaints did not amount to collective bargaining issues or involve violations of any laws or regulations. They were more like, "Marcia's talking behind my back. My supervisor won't tell her to stop!"

(continued)

(continued)

In that organization, it was expected that I would meet with the parties to make judgments about who was at fault (often they both were) and what each should do differently to improve the relationship going forward. Including supervisors, we would often have three or four people in these meetings. *And* this was considered a completely appropriate way to spend our time.

Does this story sound familiar?

The most glaring problem with this approach is that *it does more harm than good*. There is a lot of finger pointing, and all the focus on the problem magnifies the negativity. When the meeting is over, everyone feels worse, and the relationship is not any better. Most people in this situation are completely unconscious of this reality. They just keep doing it.

As a manager, if you are mediating relationships in this way, you are enabling employees to avoid speaking directly to each other about their issues. You are allowing them to transfer to you the responsibility of solving their interpersonal problems. You can make a different choice. You can stop investing time mediating relationships.

This kind of interpersonal conflict can and should become a coaching opportunity, focused on helping your people solve their own problems. You can insist that they speak directly to each other, without third parties involved. If they need help with strategies for having those difficult conversations, you can help them. But don't do it for them.

LESSON

If you stop mediating relationships, you will:

1. Stop making things worse.
2. Invest more time on things that actually add value.
3. Cultivate a culture in which people know how to resolve interpersonal problems, maybe even before they become problems.

That is a win/win/win strategy.

EXPERIMENT: QUIT MEDIATING RELATIONSHIPS

1. The next time someone asks you to mediate a relationship, recognize it for what it is and politely decline.
2. Tell the people involved that they need to talk to each other and work it out.
3. Repeat steps one and two every time you are asked to mediate a relationship.
4. After 30 days, think about those situations. Are the relationships better, worse, or about the same? How do you feel about not getting involved with all that drama?

We mentioned that this should become a coaching opportunity. You will inevitably find people who have no idea how to go about solving interpersonal conflicts with colleagues. You can help by coaching them on building trust. If you struggle with managing conflict yourself, this next section can help you and the people you manage develop some positive strategies.

TRUST AND CONFLICT—YOU CAN TAKE THE FIRST STEP

Conflict is inevitable, and there is no one-size-fits-all approach to dealing with it because not every situation involves the same variables. The people on both sides of a conflict might have different strengths (and weaknesses) in working through the situation, and they might have different preferred approaches. Their intent might differ. They might seek different goals. The conflict itself might have a different meaning to each person. There is, however, one variable that has the greatest impact on the situation: your relationship with the other person.

The higher the level of mutual trust, the easier it is to agree on a constructive solution. Conflicts are most easily resolved among genuine friends. But if you doubt the other person's motives, trust is definitely low. If you do not know each other well, trust might be low. When trust is low, we are frequently mistaken in our assumptions about the other person's intent.

Think about this hypothetical situation that, sadly, is all too common. Suppose you have to work with someone you believe (perhaps for *very* good reasons) intentionally does things to undermine you. Trust is low. In the normal course of business, he calls a meeting and does not include you, even though you clearly should have been invited. Before reading further, take a moment to answer the following questions:

- How does that make you feel?
- How will you respond?

Now, alter that hypothetical slightly. Suppose a *close friend* at work calls a meeting and does not include you, even though you clearly should have been invited.

- How does that make you feel?
- How will you respond?

There is a good chance that your answers for the first hypothetical were very different from your answers for the second one.

In the first hypothetical, you might be upset or even angry. Depending on your style, you might confront that person in an adversarial manner. Or you might not discuss it directly with the person but instead discuss it with others, as more evidence that this person is trying to undermine you. Neither response is constructive.

In the second hypothetical you might be somewhat upset, but your response would not be adversarial, and you certainly would not badmouth your close friend. You would be more likely to have a nonconfrontational conversation about why you were not invited, and you might even start from the assumption that it was an oversight. Your response would be constructive.

When trust is low, we automatically attribute bad motives. When trust is high we refuse to believe that bad motives account for the behavior. *But* your assumptions about a person's motives might be mistaken. It is almost always constructive to ask why the person behaved as he or she did . . . *if* you ask the way you would ask your close friend.

As Stephen R. Covey said, "Seek first to understand, then to be understood." You want to get better at resolving conflict? Cultivate your active listening skills. Through active listening, you will discover the other person's perspectives and concerns about the situation, which sets the stage for constructive resolution. You will be surprised at how frequently you discover your assumptions about the other's intent were wrong.

Furthermore, you must be open and honest about *your* intent, your goals, and your concerns. As best-selling author Dr. Dan Baker taught me, high mutual disclosure builds trust.

LESSON

- Your interpretation of someone's behavior depends on your relationship with that person.
- When trust is low, be aware that your assumptions about that person's motives might be wrong.

- Demonstrate your sincere intent to understand the other person's point of view.
- Recognize that your feelings do not have to dictate your behavior.

EXPERIMENT: CHOOSE TRUSTING BEHAVIORS

1. Be alert for the next situation in which someone you don't fully trust does something you don't like.
2. Ask yourself, "Suppose the person who did this (whatever "this" is) were my best friend. How would I respond? What would I do?"
3. Choose that behavior, even if it makes you uncomfortable.
4. Continue to choose trusting behaviors with others.
5. After 90 days, think about what impact you have had on others and how this has affected you.

In the case of being excluded from a meeting, for example, start with the assumption that it was an oversight (even if you do not believe it!) and choose your behavior based on that assumption. We are not suggesting that this strategy is easy to implement. It is difficult because . . . well . . . you do not trust that person. It involves risk, and it requires you to be the bigger person.

The final point about resolving conflict is challenging for many people.

LESSON

Sometimes you need to set aside your pride and your need to be right.

Sometimes the best move to resolve a conflict is to apologize even when you did not do anything wrong. If you can let go of your need to be right, you will be amazed at how many conflicts are rapidly resolved.

A friend, Carol Ott Schacht, sums up this strategy quite eloquently: "Love 'em to goodness."

Chapter 9

APOLOGIZE

Plenty of managers just can't bring themselves to admit when they have screwed up in some way. Have you ever worked with a manager like this? Because they are in a position of power, everyone who reports to managers who can't apologize adjusts to it. They have no choice. These leaders just cannot say, "I'm sorry." It's one thing to have power. It's another thing how you use it.

What kind of manager are you? If you make a wrong decision, if you are in error, do you own it? Do you apologize? Do you make amends? Or . . . are you the type of manager who wants to hold employees accountable but will not be accountable to your employees? It's not clear what is gained by this behavior, but here's what is lost: respect and moral authority. Your employees are not under the delusion that you have no flaws or that you make no errors. But if you do not own your errors, they will draw the conclusion that *you* are under that delusion. Thus the loss of respect and credibility.

Think about customers for a minute. When you are dealing with upset customers, and you are trying to make them happy, you know that in many cases just saying, "I'm sorry," *and meaning it* is all those customers need. Horst Schulze taught this lesson:

> "Guest satisfaction is not about whether you spill the soup on the guest. It's about what you do after you spill the soup."

A service recovery situation gives you the opportunity to demonstrate how much you care. In some cases, your relationship will actually be better after the unfortunate event. Of course, you want to fix whatever went wrong, but with customers, sincerely apologizing almost always improves the situation. We have made numerous apologies to customers, sometimes even when we did not do anything wrong. You have done this, too. Why? Not because the customer is always right. We do it to retain the customer. We want the relationship to continue. *We want our customers to know we sincerely care about them.*

Have you considered the fact that, as a manager, your employees are now your most important customers? Do you treat them the same way you would treat customers? Be the kind of manager who apologizes when you make a mistake or when you fail people in some way. And deliver the kind of apology that will likely make the biggest difference.

There are definitely better and worse apologies. Asking for forgiveness and stopping there is in the "worse" category. In fact, it is the least effective way to apologize, maybe because merely asking for forgiveness represents nothing more than additional cost to the person you have wronged. Better apologies happen when you shift the cost away from the person you have wronged and own that cost yourself. The two most effective elements of an apology are (Lewicki, 2016):[1]

1. Acknowledging responsibility
2. Making an offer of repair

People want to hear you own it (whatever *it* is), and they want you to make a commitment to fix it or to compensate them for it. When you do those two things, you begin to bear some of the cost of your mistake. And when you go on from there to express genuine regret, explain what went wrong, promise sincerely to do better in the future (and then ask for forgiveness), you give people the kind of comprehensive apology that makes a difference in the relationship—the kind of apology that makes it possible for the relationship to be even stronger after the unfortunate event.

But what about times when you have not done anything wrong and someone still wants an apology? What then?

The Unintended Insult

At one point in my career, I was the manager of a team of consultants at Talent Plus. We were genuine road warriors, routinely traveling three weeks per month—or more. To help new employees learn about our business, we were asked to make a brief video about what our team did. I enlisted a group of four consultants to make this video, and because we were road warriors we recorded the video at the airport.

In the course of explaining what we did, one of the consultants thanked another team who provided significant support for arranging travel and liaising with clients to ensure consulting visits accomplished their goals.

When that team viewed our video, they became upset. They thought we had trivialized their role. Their supervisor delivered this message to me, and I immediately offered to apologize publicly and to delete those remarks from the video.

I made this offer despite the fact that I knew we didn't do anything wrong. In my opinion, they should not have been upset. We were sincerely thanking them for their support. However, from their point of view, we had wronged them and they deserved an apology.

I decided to validate their feelings and *operate from their point of view*. I delivered my public apology and deleted the thank you from the video. My relationship with that team was more important to me than being right.

LESSON

Being right is highly overrated. If someone believes you have wronged them, operate from their point of view. Apologizing improves the situation, gains respect, and adds to your moral authority. Most importantly, it demonstrates that you truly care more about the other person than about being right.

EXPERIMENT: APOLOGIZE

1. Identify a situation in which you made a mistake or otherwise did something wrong.
2. Apologize, paying special attention to acknowledging responsibility and making an offer of repair.
3. Pay attention to how rapidly things improve.

Chapter 10

FORGIVE

What happens when you are on the other side of an apology, in the position to forgive someone who has wronged you in some way? For a manager, the opportunity to forgive most commonly arises when an employee has screwed up. She has done something you, as her manager, perceive to be mistaken, wrong, or otherwise unacceptable. Assume that this mistake is not trivial. It causes a significant problem in the business, and maybe it even hurts you personally. The following example involves possibly the biggest screw-up of Larry's professional career.

Larry Embarrasses His Boss

My boss and mentor at that time was Phil Lombardi, VP of HR for Hyatt Hotels. He gave me the assignment to create a video training program for employees, which he would present at the company's annual general managers meeting. I hired outside experts to write, direct, and produce this video and the accompanying training materials.

When Phil presented the program, the general managers universally hated it. To a person, they stated emphatically that they would not implement this program in their hotels. When I recovered from the shock, at the earliest opportunity, I tendered my resignation to Phil. He told me he had just tendered his resignation to the president. The president did not accept Phil's resignation and Phil did not accept mine. He forgave me, and *he never mentioned it again.*

Forgiveness does not require you to forget the act or deny that it was wrong. It involves letting go of resentment and thoughts of revenge. Fred Luskin is a pioneer in the science and practice of forgiveness and leader of the Stanford Forgiveness Projects. He describes forgiveness as "resilience in the face of unwanted outcomes."[1] The issue is less about forgetting and more about letting go of all the negative feelings we experience when things do not go the way we want.

If you do not forgive, the negative feelings you retain will infect your relationships with the people involved and taint the way you treat each other, thereby undermining success for both of you. Furthermore, holding a grudge is bad for your health.[2] Just thinking about an old grudge increases physical responses like blood pressure, heart rate, and muscle tension and leads people to feel angrier, more anxious, and less in control. By contrast, just thinking about forgiving (or at least empathizing with) someone who has wronged you reverses those physical effects and diminishes the feelings that go along with them.[3]

In case being healthier and feeling better is not motivation enough, forgiveness can actually increase productivity and performance in a business setting. In a study that began after the stock market crash of 2000, Luskin's team provided training on emotional competence and forgiveness to financial advisors working for American Express Financial Services. Participants in the training increased their sales by 25 percent—more than double the 10 percent increase their peers who did not participate achieved over the same period.[4] More recent research concurs that forgiveness in the workplace is linked to increased productivity, decreased absenteeism, fewer mental and physical health problems, better decision making, improved cognitive functioning and higher quality of relationships while holding on to grudges is associated with higher aggression, lower collaboration, and greater disengagement.[5]

All the evidence converges on the idea that forgiveness makes a positive difference for everyone involved—even for the bottom line. Look, we are all going to screw up at times. We are human beings, for goodness sake. We all need forgiveness. And the research shows that we are all better off when we learn how to forgive. Holding a grudge comes at a cost. You will be seen as petty and mean-spirited. You will drive up turnover, diminish collaboration, undermine your chances for success, and put your own health at risk. Who needs that? Life is short. Whatever it is, get over it. Let it go. Everyone will be glad you did, especially you.

The weak can never forgive. Forgiveness is an attribute of the strong.

—Mahatma Gandhi

LESSON

As a manager, when you forgive, you increase loyalty and appreciation from others, increase your moral authority, model truly exemplary behavior, improve your relationships, improve your health, and increase your chances for success. Who wouldn't want all that?

EXPERIMENT: FORGIVE

1. Identify someone you have not forgiven for something.
2. When negativity about how you have been wronged creeps into your thoughts, let go of your resentment. Think about something else and move on with life. Let go of that negativity. It's hurting you and nobody else.

CULTIVATE A GREAT RELATIONSHIP WITH YOUR BOSS

Though the lessons and experiments we have shared in this section have focused on how to cultivate great relationships with the people you manage, most of them can apply to any relationship, even your relationship with your boss. Because managing up is a very important part of almost everyone's life, it is important to devote some time to the question, "How do I cultivate a great relationship with my boss?"

Larry's best friend, the late Pat Mene, was a top performer, whose expertise and leadership won two Malcolm Baldridge Awards for The Ritz-Carlton Hotel Company. Pat was a great manager in his own right, and based on some of the "managing up" he experienced, he created a list of the top-10 ass-kissing lines of all time. Number one on the list: "Boss, now I know how the disciples must have felt!" Ass kissing is a time-honored approach to managing up, but we do not recommend it. We do not recommend self-promotion or manipulation. We recommend investing in the relationship, and we will share some specific suggestions with you here. To get us started, here is a story from Kim:

Kim Makes a Difference

One of the best relationships I have ever had with a leader started with me going to him after a meeting in which he lost his temper and people left with hurt feelings. He was not himself. I gave it a day to settle and the next day

(continued)

51

(*continued*)

walked into his office, sat down across from him and asked, "How are you? Is everything okay?" That question was disarming, and it resulted in a great discussion. He told me later that in 20 years of leadership, nobody on his staff had ever done that for him, and it was one crucial interaction that cemented trust and helped us become a powerful leadership team.

LESSON

Your boss is a person! Genuine caring will make a big difference in his or her life, too.

Here are some guidelines to help you manage up.

1. Accept your boss as she is. Honor her character traits, values, strengths, and weaknesses. Do not try to change her. Just as this is the cornerstone of cultivating positive relationships with the people you manage, this may be the single-most-affirming thing you can do for your boss.
2. Look for areas in which you and the boss have complementary strengths. These present opportunities for synergy.
3. Look for areas in which you have strengths that are weaknesses for your boss. These are unique ways you can help him.
4. Look for areas in which your boss has strengths and you have potential but lack experience. Ask her to help you grow in these areas.
5. Make your boss's priorities your own.* Understand his needs, goals, and expectations. You want to understand these things about your customers, don't you? Why? Because knowing these things empowers you to add value *as your customer defines it.* Do the same for your boss. The more clarity you have about his expectations, the easier it is to meet (and exceed) those expectations.
6. Demonstrate fierce loyalty and unmitigated trust. Make sure your boss knows you seek her greatest good. Keep your boss well informed. Do not hide information. Be willing to ask tough questions and share things that are true, even if she might not want to hear them. When you disagree with decisions she has made, do it in private. Support the decisions in

---

*Thanks to my former boss and mentor, Sigi Brauer, for this piece of wisdom. That one sentence has helped many of his former direct reports.

public, even if you do not agree. Remember, you might be wrong. Do not speak negatively about your boss to others. That is blatantly disloyal. If you are going to meet with your boss's boss, say so before you do it. If her boss calls you into a meeting unexpectedly, let your boss know what it was about as soon as possible.

7. Ask for advice and guidance. Although you should bring possible solutions, you will run into problems. It shows respect to ask your boss for guidance.

8. Do not be defensive. That is worth repeating. Do not be defensive. Start from a position of trust, assuming that your boss seeks your greatest good. From time to time, you are going to have your ass chewed. Sometimes it will be unfair. As a friend, Jim Horsman, says, "Lick your wounds and move on."

9. Share good news. Do not create a situation in which you only interact with your boss when there is a problem or when you are going to ask for something. Share a team success, share something great about one of your team members, or share a new idea.

10. Show appreciation. Give your boss recognition when he has earned it. We tend to think about recognition as being only top down. We need to escape that thinking. Like anyone else in your organization, your boss does things that merit some recognition. It does not have to be expensive or time consuming.

Managing up effectively makes a difference in your relationship with your manager. Also consider this: The way you manage up sets a powerful example for the people you manage. Are you managing up with your leader in the way you would like your team members to manage up with you? In closing this chapter, we leave you with this question: On a scale from 1 to 10, how much does your boss enjoy spending time with you? Know the answer to this question, and try these suggestions for pushing that number up.

EXPERIMENT: MANAGE UP

1. Review the guidelines listed in this chapter and rate your effectiveness on each, using a 1-to-10 scale, with 10 indicating "excellent" and 1 indicating "terrible."
2. Pick one or two guidelines and work on improving in those areas.
3. In 30 days, rate yourself again on all guidelines.

What did you learn?

EMBRACE THE EBB AND FLOW OF RELATIONSHIPS

Cultivating positive relationships makes a difference. We have given you a number of experiments to test out in your laboratory that can help you cultivate more positive relationships—with the people you manage, with your own manager, and even with your friends and family. Here is an important caveat. In any relationship, things are not always equal, and that can lead you to feel dissatisfied. If you let it.

Many of us carry around the notion that relationships between two people should be 50/50. In the ideal scenario, the burdens should be shared equally, and so should the rewards. While that would be nice, that is not reality. In reality, on any given day, one person in the relationship puts in more and carries more of the burden, even though the rewards are equally shared. Relationships have an ebb and flow. They may be 60/40 in one direction on some days and 70/30 in the opposite direction on other days. *And* this might *not* even out over time. But the rewards might be equally shared anyway. Is this fair? Is this equitable? Interestingly, yes.

As a manager, you have separate one-on-one relationships with each of your direct reports. And each person has different needs. One, for example, needs public recognition. Another needs to vent every other day. A third needs strong, clear direction and follow-up. Great managers put the needs of their people ahead of their own needs. Great managers understand that often they must do more of the relationship "heavy lifting" to help their people thrive.

This ebb and flow also exists in your personal relationships. On any given day, the contributions from each person will not be 50/50. During a given period of time, more might be asked of you. You might have to be more forgiving, more courageous, or more disciplined. In any relationship, each person brings different needs and capabilities to the ebb and flow. It is extremely unlikely each person will contribute equally. Do not seek equity. Just ask yourself the following question:

"Is the value I am getting out of this relationship worth what I am putting into it?"

In all cases, personal and professional, you need to be clear about *why* you are in the relationship. Because the "why" informs the value you receive. Value, like beauty, is in the eye of the beholder. Once you are clear about the *why*, you can answer that question. It bears repeating:

"Is the value I am getting out of this relationship worth what I am putting into it?"

If your answer is, "Yes," why worry about whether the other person is getting more than they deserve based on what they are putting into the relationship? If their rewards were reduced, how would that help you? Why not have an abundance mentality?

If your answer is, "No. What I am getting is not worth what I am putting into it," make a change. If you cannot—or will not—change your relationship, then accept it and embrace it. Stress arises from resistance to what is.

LESSON

Don't seek a 50/50 balance in any relationship. That is not reality. Let it go. Have an abundance mentality. Embrace the ebb and flow.

EXPERIMENT: EVALUATE A DIFFICULT RELATIONSHIP

1. Identify a relationship you find unsatisfying.
2. Write notes about what you are putting into that relationship (the cost) and what you are getting out of it (the reward).
3. Decide: If nothing changes, is what I am getting worth what it is costing me?
4. If yes, accept that it is not a 50/50 relationship. Quit resenting or complaining.
5. If no, make a change.
   a. If you are not willing to make a change in the relationship, that is okay. But understand your unwillingness as a signal that you really *do*

think what you're getting is worth putting up with what you don't like. So at least embrace that and change the way you are thinking about the relationship.

b. If you are genuinely unable to change the relationship, do the same thing. Accept it, embrace it, and change the way you think about it.

6. Whatever your decision, consider the value of forgiveness—resilience in the face of unwanted outcomes. Even if no apology will ever be forthcoming, forgiveness has the power to positively affect you and the relationship.

ACCELERATE PEOPLE'S GROWTH

ABANDON THE "FOLLOW SHIRLEY" METHOD

You are still reading because you want to manage in a way that really makes a difference—for your employees and for your organization. We have spent a lot of time talking about how you can cultivate the positive relationships that will enhance your understanding of people and your ability to influence their performance, engagement, and retention. Now we are going to get really practical about specific ways you can push people's growth further and faster.

Begin at the beginning—on an employee's first day with you. That is your first opportunity to influence and accelerate growth. Are you making the most of it?

Follow Shirley

Over the years, I have worked with a number of hospitality and retail companies, and I have found that one of the most common approaches to that first day is the "Follow Shirley" method. Here's how it goes.

Day One. A new employee appears in a department at the beginning of the shift. In some cases, the department head has not been informed to expect this new person. In other cases, they expect the new person, but they have not had time to prepare because they are short-staffed and very busy. So the manager says, "Glad to see you! Follow Shirley today to learn about your new job."

The new person follows Shirley and at best learns what Shirley happens to be doing that day. That's at best. In many cases, however, Shirley does not have a positive attitude. In those cases, this brand new,

(continued)

(continued)

highly impressionable employee also learns, from Shirley, why this is such a crappy place to work.

Day Two. It is Shirley's day off. The new employee now follows Jose. In reference to what the new employee learned from Shirley, Jose says, "That's not the way we do it. This is the right way to do that." At the end of the day, the new person has not made much progress, feels pretty confused, and is beginning to wonder what she's gotten into.

Here is the alternative. First, think about why you selected Shirley as the trainer.

- Because she was simply available at the time?
- Because she is the best performer on your team?
- Because she is the highest seniority person?

None of these are good reasons. To decide who should teach and coach this new employee, choose the best teacher and coach. This sounds obvious. But if it were obvious, nobody would be using the Follow Shirley method. As you go about choosing your best teacher and coach, remember that the best performer is often not the best teacher. Doing something well and teaching others how to do it are two entirely different endeavors, and they require different talents.

LESSON

When choosing someone to train new employees, choose the best teacher and coach. The best teacher and coach may not be the best performer on your team.

How can you tell who is the best teacher and coach? First, choose someone who has a strong, positive attitude. A negative trainer will poison new employees from day one. Next, pay attention to which employees are teaching and coaching others spontaneously, even though it is not their job. They can't not do it, and they will love having the responsibility of doing it with new people.

Help your trainer by preparing a checklist of learning goals. This checklist should answer the following question: "What should a new employee know and be able to do in order to perform in this role up to my standards?" Don't create a big, honking training manual. Just make a list. This accomplishes a couple of important goals. First, it creates consistency. Every trainer uses the same list.

Furthermore, there will be items on that list that will not come up in a normal day of following Shirley. For example, what should you do in the case of a fire?

EXPERIMENT: IMPLEMENT A BETTER TRAINING PROCESS

1. Identify employees who have strong positive attitudes and who enjoy teaching and coaching.
2. Make a list of items to be learned.
3. Make sure everyone involved in training new employees works from this list.
4. Instruct the new employee to check off each item as it is learned. This way, you can check progress even if you are not personally training the new employee.
5. After you have used this approach with three new hires, reflect on what you have learned. Are they getting up to speed faster? How do the trainers feel about it? Can you improve the list?

HELP PEOPLE SELF-ACTUALIZE

The definition of self-actualization is simple and straightforward. To self-actualize is to realize or to fulfill your talent and potential. Self-actualization, like significance, is a fundamental human drive. While defining it is simple, achieving self-actualization is nothing short of profound. As a manager, you have a unique opportunity to help people self-actualize. How can you make the most of this opportunity?

The Bellman and the Pizza

In 1989, I was on the opening team for The Ritz-Carlton, Dearborn, not too far from Detroit. About a week before opening, around 7 PM, I happened to be at the employee entrance when a pizza delivery guy arrived with a couple of pizzas. Just as he arrived, a bellman came around the corner and asked if he could have one of the pizzas. The delivery guy asked, "Are you Mr. Johnson?" The bellman replied, "No, I'm not, but I really need one of those pizzas."

He explained that his supervisor had asked him to work through dinner, which was served from 4 to 6 PM in the employee dining room. He had no money to buy dinner and no transportation home. Even though it was not open yet, he would stay in the hotel overnight. He told the pizza delivery guy that he would not have anything to eat until morning. As I watched this interaction unfold, the bellman actually persuaded the delivery guy to give him a pizza.

(continued)

(*continued*)

Once he had the pizza, he walked off and I followed him around the corner. There were two other bellmen waiting for him. They were in the same situation. The pizza would feed all three of them.

The next morning, I got a call from the hotel general manager, who said, "Larry, I understand you witnessed Tyrone (the bellman's name) steal a pizza last night. We are going to take disciplinary action and we need you to state what you saw." It turned out that the pizza was for a big vice president, Mr. Johnson, who was really angry.

I said, "I saw the incident, but there was no stealing. Tyrone just talked the guy into giving him a pizza. It was very impressive. I don't think he should be disciplined." The general manager asked me what I thought should happen. I said, "What I saw last night was leadership talent. He was taking care of his team. I think you should put him in the management training program."

They agreed to do that and Tyrone continued to impress people with his effectiveness.

The best managers help people self-actualize. They receive a great deal of intrinsic satisfaction from helping others explore and make progress on their potential. The first step in this process is to spot talent. By "talent" we mean aptitude or giftedness—the potential to do something with excellence. I was able to spot Tyrone's leadership talent, and that was the first step in providing him an opportunity to self-actualize.

Think about parenting for a moment. Wise parents involve their children in many different activities. Why? They are looking for activities each child seems to enjoy.

If a person (adult or child) naturally enjoys a certain activity, he or she *will* want to do more of it. As that person does more of that activity, it will become clear over time whether he or she has the talent to perform with excellence.

So, whether you are a manager or a parent who wants to help someone self-actualize, how do you spot this kind of potential so you can provide opportunities for it to develop? Look for:

Yearning For reasons that need not be explained, the person wants to try some activity. She thinks it just looks fun and interesting. It calls to her. Who cares why? This desire often occurs as a result of watching someone else do it with excellence. When you notice this yearning, find a way to give her a taste.

Flashes of Brilliance You see instances of extraordinary performance—sometimes just flashes—that are not due to luck. Tyrone's performance is a great example. The first time it might look like luck, but if you see something that looks like beginner's luck—*pay attention!!* Do not blithely attribute it to luck. Be curious. Get the person more involved in this activity to see if more flashes of brilliance occur.

Rapid Learning and Progress This activity just seems to come naturally to the person. Learning is fun and easy. Progress is more rapid (sometimes *much* more rapid) than average. The person is convinced that he will achieve greater levels of performance with additional opportunities to practice. Often, the person knows, "I can *do* this!" Tyrone made extremely rapid progress as a manager.

Joy The person just *loves* doing this activity. It resonates with something inside her. She gains positive energy from it and looks forward to her next opportunity to do it.

When you see these signs of potential, invest the time and effort to explore it. Allow people the opportunity to self-actualize because self-actualizing equals growth. And when people are growing, morale, engagement, and retention improve. When people are growing, the overall value they add to your organization increases. When people are growing, all stakeholders benefit.

In your role as a manager, spotting potential (then doing something about it) is one of the best ways to make sure people are growing. And that makes a difference for them and for your organization.

LESSON

To help a person self-actualize, begin by understanding his or her talents. Look for a yearning to try something, flashes of brilliance, rapid learning, and joy in the doing.

Once you have identified a talent in someone, you can apply the GIFT Formula.

This formula describes a powerful way to help people grow and self-actualize. Here is the formula:

$$(\textbf{Talent} + \textbf{Fit}) \times \textbf{Investment} = \textbf{Growth}^{\circledR}$$

We often abbreviate it as $(T + F) \times I = G$. The abbreviation spells GIFT backward.

The story about Tyrone illustrates the first step in the formula, spotting a talent. If you want to help someone grow, you must first recognize her talent. What is she naturally good at? What does she enjoy doing? Where do you see yearning to learn, flashes of brilliance, and rapid progress? Where does she experience joy? This is the place to start, because, according to the formula, when talent is higher, the potential for growth is higher.

The next element of the formula is Fit. People are in the right Fit when their areas of potential for excellence (their talents) align with their responsibilities, the metrics for their success, and the culture of the organization. If you do not get the Fit right, people will grow less, and be at a higher risk of failing at the job, even if their talent is high.

The Entrepreneur and the Bureaucracy

The CEO of a large insurance company asked me to evaluate a candidate for president of an HMO (health maintenance organization). The successful candidate would report directly to the CEO. This particular candidate, Rebecca, was very impressive. She had built and sold two HMOs. She was experienced, knowledgeable, and talented.

I called the CEO and said, "I have good news and bad news. The good news is that Rebecca's a terrific candidate. The bad news is that she is very entrepreneurial. She moves fast and likes to call her own shots. Your company is extremely bureaucratic, which will stifle her. She can do a terrific job, but only if you free her from the bureaucracy. You have to let her do her own thing."

The CEO called me back three days later and said, "I think I'm going to pass. I wish we could accommodate someone like her, but we *are* bureaucratic and I don't think we'll be able to make the necessary accommodations."

That was the right call. Despite her obvious talent, Rebecca was not a good fit. She would not have enjoyed working in that culture, and she would not have been good at navigating their bureaucracy.

The third element of the GIFT Formula is Investment. Once you have understood a person's talent and put him or her in the right fit for that talent, the proper kind of investment will result in remarkable growth. Investment takes many forms, including training, mentoring, and assigning new responsibilities. People can invest in themselves but more often the investment comes from their managers. Notice in the formula that Investment is a multiplier. Remember your second-grade math; anything times zero equals zero. You can take all the talent in the world and create the perfect fit, but if there is zero investment, you can expect zero growth. Alternatively, maximize talent, fit, and investment, and you will maximize growth.

Putting It All Together: (T + F) × I = G

When I was opening The Ritz-Carlton Millennia Singapore, the company was into Total Quality Management (TQM), and process improvement was a major strategic area of focus. So I was looking for someone to lead our process improvement efforts. A young man named Bruce came to my attention. Although he had not formally served in that kind of role, several things in his interview suggested that he had the talent for it, and his themes were a good fit for the organization.

Even though he had no previous experience, I decided to bet on Bruce's talent and invest the resources necessary to train him in Ritz-Carlton's approach to TQM. As part of that investment, the vice president of quality, Pat Mene, came to Singapore to train Bruce personally, one-on-one. At the conclusion of his visit, Pat told me Bruce was the best student he had ever taught.

Bruce grew rapidly in that role, and made numerous important contributions to the success of that hotel.

LESSON

To help people grow:

- Understand their talent.
- Determine the best fit.
- Invest in growth activities in their areas of true potential.

EXPERIMENT: APPLY THE GIFT FORMULA

1. Do this with each of your direct reports, starting with your best performer.
2. List the things they are good at and enjoy. Take note of areas in which you see a yearning to try something, flashes of brilliance, rapid learning, and joy in the doing.
3. Find ways to invest in one or more of those areas.
4. After 90 days, see what you have learned. How has each person grown? What is their engagement like? How does this make you feel?

COACH TO IMPROVE PERFORMANCE

In addition to helping people self-actualize (which is a long-term process), managers must also coach people to improve their performance in the short term. Many managers used to do the job of the people they are coaching, and based on their past success they believe they know *the* way to achieve success. Many sales training programs are based on this sort of belief. The limitation of this approach to coaching is this: It does not occur to the coach that others may not be capable of demonstrating the recommended behaviors.

If you are coaching someone remember this: Just because you were (or are) capable of doing something, that does not mean the person you are coaching possesses those same capabilities. Of course, there are some behaviors you can teach. But managers routinely make two mistakes:

1. They assume that what comes naturally to them comes naturally to everyone.
2. They overestimate their ability to help others demonstrate behaviors that are not aligned with their themes.

Those mistakes are not consistent with accepting people as they are. As a manager, if you do make those mistakes you are not optimizing all the elements of the GIFT Formula.

For example, if a person is not good at telling jokes, coaching him to tell a joke at the beginning of a speech will not improve his performance. In all likelihood, he will tell it poorly. People will not laugh, and it will make things worse. A great coach will help the person identify a different way to begin a speech, an approach that aligns with his talent and involves behaviors he can do naturally. As Peter

71

Drucker advised, "Build the strengths and make the weaknesses irrelevant." Find ways to work around weaknesses.

Larry Coaches the Restaurant Manager

During the pre-opening training period of The Ritz-Carlton, Laguna Niguel, Andy, the fine dining restaurant manager, asked me for some tips on how to become a better public speaker. His wait staff was starting in a couple of days and he was quite concerned about his capability as a teacher. He said, "I'm a one-on-one guy. I'm great at training people one-on-one, but I'm not comfortable in front of a group." I asked if he had an assistant manager who was a good group teacher. As it happened, his assistant really enjoyed group training.

I said, "Here's what you do. Give only one speech to the group. Go up there and say, 'Hi, I'm Andy. I'm looking forward to spending a lot of time training each of you one-on-one in the restaurant. Let me introduce you to Carl, our assistant restaurant manager. Carl is a great teacher, and he'll be conducting your group training sessions.' Don't worry about being a better public speaker. That's not your thing."

Andy looked like the weight of the world was just taken off his shoulders. He took my advice and the training was very successful. By the way, he also made an investment in Carl's growth by giving him a chance to take on new responsibilities in an area that was a perfect fit for his talent as a teacher and trainer. Win-win.

LESSON

Don't worry so much about how *you* would do it. Each person creates success by using his or her unique configuration of strengths. As a coach, you must understand that there are many paths to success. If you want to be a great coach, you must grow beyond helping others understand how you achieved success. You must help them figure out how *they* are going to achieve success.

Furthermore, great coaches focus on specific, actionable recommendations rather than talking in generalities. For example, instead of saying, "You have to be a better listener," a great coach might say, "When the prospect is talking, don't interrupt. Take notes if you can."

The best coaches invest more time reviewing successful performances than they spend reviewing failures. If you want to learn more about failure, study failure. If you want to learn more about success, study success.

Coaching is an ongoing, everyday responsibility. Do not confine your coaching feedback to annual or semi-annual reviews. Conduct CIDs frequently, and use them as individualized coaching opportunities. Give people frequent, candid feedback—in real time. Do not shy away from tough conversations.

LESSON

1. Focus on building strengths rather than eliminating weaknesses.
2. Find workarounds for weaknesses.
3. Study successful performances to learn how to repeat those performances.
4. Provide specific rather than general recommendations.
5. Provide frequent, candid feedback in real time.

EXPERIMENT: BECOME A BETTER COACH

1. Don't focus on how *you* create success. Help each person have insight about how *to* use *his or her unique* strengths to create success.
2. Focus on building strengths rather than eliminating weaknesses.
3. Find workarounds for weaknesses. (Review Andy's story from this chapter for an example.)
4. Study successful performances to learn how to repeat those performances.
5. Provide specific rather than general recommendations.
6. Provide frequent, candid feedback in real time.
7. After 90 days, reflect on what you have learned. How much improvement did you see in people's performance? How did the coaching process feel to you? How did it feel to those you coached?

OPTIMIZE FIT

I f your goal is to accelerate people's growth, it is critical to optimize fit. We touched on this idea in the previous chapters. Aligning expectations to people's talents and themes creates optimal fit, and optimal fit increases the power of any investment you make in people's growth. This is so important to accelerating people's growth that we are unpacking it a little further in this chapter. Here is a story to get us started:

The Scorpion and the Frog

A scorpion and a frog were chatting on the riverbank. The scorpion wanted to go to the other side of the river, but scorpions cannot swim. So he asked the frog for a lift.

Scorpion: "I want to cross to the other side. Will you give me a lift? I can ride on your back if you'll let me."

Frog: "I am afraid you'll sting me and I'll die."

Scorpion: "Why would I do that? If I sting you, we'll both die!"

Frog: "That makes sense. Okay, hop on."

Halfway across the river, the scorpion stings the frog.

Frog, with his last breath: "Why did you do that? Now we're both going to die!"

Scorpion, with his last breath, said: "I'm a scorpion. It's my nature."

LESSON

There are things a person can't do.
There are things a person can do.
There are things a person will do.
There are things a person can't *not* do.

Scorpion can't swim. And he can't *not* sting. Is there another way to get him across the river? Is there a way to get him across the river that aligns with something he can do or will do or can't *not* do to achieve the goal?

As a manager, do your expectations of others match their themes? Are you asking people for behaviors they do not have in their repertoires? What will happen if you change your expectations so that they align with people's themes?

The Public Relations Director and the Company President

I was hiring a public relations professional for Monarch Hotels. I found a candidate, Oliver, with excellent experience and great references. Our interviews with him went exceedingly well. All lights were green with one exception: He took a lot of time to process things before he would deliver a result. And this theme was so strong in him that he considered it unethical to do work too rapidly because he could not produce high enough quality when he felt rushed.

The president of the company, Sigi Brauer, was a very impatient individual. He wanted things done immediately or faster. I explained to Sigi, "Here's the deal. This guy is an excellent PR professional, but he will take a lot more time than you like before he completes an assignment."

Sigi said, "Now that I'm aware of it, I will not react my normal way. I'll align my expectations to his themes." But Sigi couldn't do it. His own themes got in the way. He couldn't *not* be impatient. Every 90 days, I had to talk him out of firing the guy.

So we came up with a workaround designed to honor both Sigi's impatience and Oliver's reluctance to rush his work.

Sigi instructed Oliver to hire an outside PR agency. When Sigi wanted something overnight, it was Oliver's decision whether to farm it out to the agency or not. The deadline was not negotiable. Overnight meant overnight. Oliver got to decide whether he would do the assignment or not. Interestingly, when we created space for him to decide that it was okay not to do an assignment in the required time frame, Oliver actually chose more frequently to do it. But he also sometimes chose to farm it out.

We aligned expectations with both Sigi's and Oliver's themes. We did not ask either person to change. And we still got the results we needed for the business.

You get these clashes of themes sometimes, and in some cases knowing the root cause of that disharmony enables both people to manage through the situation in a more constructive way. But sometimes both people are scorpions. They just cannot help stinging each other.

You might be thinking, "Sometimes in business, people have to change or they will fail in their job." That might be true, but it does not give the person the capacity to make the required change. In fact, when you get into that kind of a situation, you probably start the kind of cycle Bill initially did with his daughter's messy room. You do not accept people as they are, you keep trying to get them to change, but they do not change. In a professional situation, you begin progressive discipline, the relationship deteriorates, and eventually the person gets fired or quits. The likely truth is that, in situations like this, the person was in the wrong job at the outset. You had the wrong expectations for him or her.

LESSON

Don't confuse *room* for improvement with *potential* for improvement. A person is in the wrong job if the job frequently calls for behavior that does not arise naturally from his or her themes.

EXPERIMENT: IDENTIFY THE RIGHT EXPECTATIONS

1. Make a list of your expectations for your top performer.
2. Make a list of changes or improvements you would like that person to make.
3. Identify expectations that do not match his or her themes—things he or she can't or can't *not* do (for example, asking an introvert to act in a more extroverted way).

(continued)

(*continued*)

4. In areas in which people's themes do not match your expectations, change your expectations.
5. For those expectations that are truly necessary for success in the job, try to think up a workaround. Look for things they naturally can and will do that will lead to their success. Or look for ways to delegate those expectations to other people who can and will get them done (Andy's story from the previous chapter and Oliver's story in this chapter are both great examples). Alternatively, work on finding that person a new job that is more aligned with who he or she is.
6. Repeat these steps for each of your direct reports.

LESSON

Quit trying to fix people. Accept them for who they are. Quit asking for behaviors they do not have in their repertoire. This will transform your relationships, and if you transform your relationships you transform your life.

We are aware that it is extremely difficult for some people to quit trying to fix others. In fact, many people will vehemently disagree with our point of view. So we ask only this. Remember that you are in a laboratory. If you believe you can fix people, pursue that strategy with conviction. Measure the outcomes of your efforts. Be aware and be honest with yourself about the results you are getting.

Chapter 17

SET THE RIGHT EXPECTATIONS

Y ou are cultivating positive relationships with your people, discovering their unique talents and strengths, optimizing the fit between their themes and their responsibilities, and working on becoming a better coach to each person on your team. What else can you do to unleash outstanding performance in the people and teams you manage? Set high expectations for their performance, make sure they are the right expectations, and communicate them in the right way. We will start with a story about how to communicate your expectations.

The Incredible Banquet Department

At The Ritz-Carlton, Tysons Corner, we had a banquet department that produced incredible results as indicated by several financial and non-financial metrics. This department had two outstanding managers—Steven Freund and Julie Naberhaus. We were presented with a wonderful problem. How do you motivate these people to achieve even better results? In many cases, a manager will say to the people, "Thank you for your great work, but we can't be satisfied. We need to do even better." There are many variations of this, and most of them send the message, "You are doing well, but you are not doing well enough."

We came up with the following alternative. After the team had achieved yet another notable success, I would visit their departmental meeting and say, "That was remarkable. You people are geniuses. I can't wait to see what you do next!" Those were very lofty expectations, articulated in a very positive way—no subtext that their performance was not good enough.

(continued)

> *(continued)*
>
> But the expectation was that they would perform like geniuses, impressing us with greater achievements. And they consistently did.

The expectations of an authority figure have powerful consequences. This phenomenon, known as the Pygmalion effect, has been thoroughly researched, beginning with Rosenthal and Jacobson's seminal study of elementary teachers and students in the 1960s[1] and continuing into J. Sterling Livingston's research as a management consultant and faculty member of the Harvard Business School.[2] The findings are remarkable and consistent whether you look at students or employees: People will live up or down to the expectations of their leader.

High expectations can drive individual growth and development. But they must be the right high expectations. They can't just be the "pie in the sky" kind. They should align with people's themes. You should not ask a person to change who they are or to achieve excellence in an area in which they do not have the appropriate themes. For example, expecting an intensely introverted person to perform with excellence in a job that requires consistent extroverted behavior is not the right expectation. But it would be the right expectation if you are dealing with an extroverted person. In the same way, your expectations for performance need to be realistic, precise, and measurable so people can know what you expect, what success looks like, and when they have hit the mark.

Here is another story about how the right high expectations created surprising success:

Marie Rises to the Challenge

I was working as a vice president of human resources for a prominent restaurant company in Chicago. Among other activities, this company had a contract to operate more than 20 restaurants in a major downtown exhibition hall. These restaurants ranged from bars to fast food to fine dining, and they opened or closed based on the conferences and exhibitions that were being conducted on any given day. So on some days, almost none of the restaurants were open and on other days they were all open and busy. There were very few full-time employees. The on-call people who staffed these restaurants were difficult to manage. Staffing and other aspects of human resources management were challenging, to say the least. Frankly, it was a nightmare.

I was very fortunate to have an administrative assistant named Marie Minarich. We had worked together for only a few months, but in that brief time I came to believe that Marie had an extraordinary amount of untapped potential. It so happened that the human resources director for the exhibition hall facility resigned, so I had to identify a replacement. Much to the surprise of the company's executives, I selected Marie. They were full of doubt because conventional wisdom suggested that this was a job for a very seasoned human resources professional.

Marie had doubts as well. Even she wasn't sure she was up to the task. But I had no doubt whatsoever. I knew she could do that job with excellence, and I told her that was what I expected. When she decided to take the job, I told the executives to just watch what happened. Marie went in there and blew it away.

Certainly, the credit goes to Marie. But it would not have happened without a manager who recognized her potential, truly believed in her ability, and placed clear expectations for her to live up to that potential.

Placing the right expectations can be one of your most satisfying activities as a leader.

Your expectations create the opportunity for people to see new possibilities. They can motivate people to achieve things they never even imagined. When you believe in your heart of hearts that people can do something, they will believe it, too. When you get this right, magic really does occur. When you do not, the Pygmalion effect can work just as strongly against success as it does for success. Remember: People will live up or down to the expectations of their leader.

So far, we have focused on the "living up" part of that idea. Beware of the "living down" part. So much of what makes the Pygmalion effect work happens in your unconscious actions.

Your expectations are communicated in a thousand ways, including tone of voice, body language, choice of words, and facial expressions. Here are some specific ways teachers, coaches, and managers might unintentionally and unconsciously act differently when they have high expectations for people to succeed:[3]

1. They create a warmer socioemotional climate through gestures as simple as a nod of the head, an encouraging smile, or a touch on the shoulder.
2. Because they have high expectations, they teach people more and provide more challenging lessons.
3. They provide more opportunities for people to contribute and provide more time for such contributions.
4. They provide personalized feedback, not just a generic pat on the back.

Those nods of the head, encouraging smiles, and touches on the shoulder encourage people to live up to your expectations—and those actions speak louder than words. But those unconscious actions only happen when you really believe people can achieve the high expectations you set for them. If, in your heart of hearts, you believe people will fail, you cannot help but behave in ways that will communicate that expectation. Those encouraging nods and smiles and pats on the back will not happen. In fact, when you believe people cannot succeed, you are prone to withdrawing and limiting your interactions with them. Silence and indifference shout that your expectations are low and you believe investments in people will yield low returns. When you really believe people cannot succeed, people will know it, and they will live down to your expectations.

LESSON

People will live up to your high and realistic expectations and they will live down to your low expectations. They will just give up on your unrealistic expectations. Above all else, you must sincerely believe that people have the capacity to live up to the expectations you set for them.

EXPERIMENT: ARTICULATE THE RIGHT EXPECTATIONS

1. Think about the potential of each employee on your team.
2. What gifts does each person have?
3. How can they use those gifts to make their best contributions to the team?
4. Give them something to live up to. Articulate some expectations in a positive way. (Review the banquet department story in this chapter.)
5. Make sure you sincerely believe they can do it.
6. See what happens.

One final thought. Think about the people who have contributed to your growth and development. Did they articulate expectations? Did they ask you to live up to your potential? How did their expectations influence your performance and growth?

ASK THE RIGHT QUESTIONS

Asking high-value questions is an art. Asking the right question is supremely important for almost any professional, including scientists, physicians, social workers, police officers, journalists, attorneys, accountants, sales professionals—the list can go on and on. The very best coaches hone and perfect the art of asking the right questions.

LESSON

- The kind of question you ask determines the kind of answer you will get.
- Asking the right question is more important than finding the answer easily. Often, the struggle to find an answer results in substantial growth.

The questions in the following experiment have served me well as a coach. But know that the *intent* of each question is more important than the question itself. If the intent is to seek the person's greatest good, that will be evident, and you will be able to ask more challenging questions. All questions are asked within the context of an existing relationship. Part of the art is understanding what questions are appropriate between you and the person you are coaching at a given point in your evolving relationship. With that understanding, here are some questions to consider if you are the coach helping someone either evaluate his or her performance or prepare for an assignment.

EXPERIMENT: REVIEW PERFORMANCE

Ask these questions to review someone's performance in a specific area in the recent past:

1. How do you think you did? (This is just to get a mental review going.)
2. Did anything surprise you?
3. What went well? And why? (People always want to focus on what did not go well. There is often more to be learned in thinking about what went well and how to repeat that in the future.)
4. What did not go so well? And why?
5. What lessons did you learn from this experience?
6. What will you do differently in the future to improve your performance? And why?

Review performance with three different people using this approach. How did it feel to you? To the other person? What did you learn about reviewing performance?

EXPERIMENT: PREPARE FOR AN UPCOMING PERFORMANCE

Ask these questions to help someone prepare for an upcoming performance event:

1. What are your desired outcomes from this event? And why?
2. How likely is it that your plan of action will achieve your desired outcomes? And why?
3. What concerns you? And why?

Help three different people prepare for an upcoming performance using these questions. How did it feel to you? To the other person? What did you learn about reviewing performance?

Part of the art of asking high-value questions is actively listening and asking great follow-up questions. Here are two follow-up questions that often add great value:

- Tell me more. (It is not technically a question, but it fulfills that purpose.)
- How can I help? (If you ask only this one question, you and everyone you coach will be well served.)

KICK BUTT THE RIGHT WAY

Kicking butt is a widespread practice that has stood the test of time. It is a valuable tool to have in your repertoire, and like any tool, you have to know how and when to use it. So kicking butt is a good idea—sometimes. It is easy to overdo this. A little goes a long way.

If kicking butt is not a natural part of your leadership style, that's okay. I advise you against trying to learn this technique or improve your use of it because there is some aptitude involved. Focus on using other techniques (those that come more naturally to you) to accomplish the same outcomes.

For you natural butt-kickers, assume your intent is to improve performance. With that worthwhile goal in mind, there are two situations in which this tool can be very effective: (1) to punish poor performance after the fact, and (2) to motivate people to create a sense of urgency.

If a person or team has performed poorly (way short of their capability), they are disappointed, and they know you are disappointed. Kicking butt brings this to closure and therefore allows you to move on. It feels appropriate to everyone. Once you have done this though, leave it behind. Do not keep punishing them.

If you are reacting to poor performance, don't kick butt when you are angry. Get beyond the anger so you can be intentional about how and when you do it.

If a person or team is not demonstrating enough urgency, kicking butt is also appropriate. This is the most easily identifiable situation in which to use this technique. This is not the only motivational technique, however. Too many leaders overuse it when other techniques might be even more effective.

It is important to understand what kicking butt can accomplish and what it cannot. It can increase someone's sense of urgency. It can make people try harder next time. It can increase their desire to perform better. But it cannot increase a person's (or a team's) level of skill or talent. Kicking butt cannot and will not increase people's ability to perform better.

If a person or team is truly giving their best, this technique will fail.

LESSON

Kicking butt cannot increase a person's ability to perform better.

It is also important to understand that when the goal is motivation, one size never fits all. The technique of kicking butt might work well on you and on some people who report to you, but it will not work for every person on your team. If it does not work for a particular employee, do not use it for that person.

In conclusion, kicking butt can be a desirable technique to have in your repertoire. However, make sure you use it only for people who respond to that particular technique, and understand what you can and can't accomplish by using it.

EXPERIMENT: KICK BUTT FOR THE RIGHT REASONS

1. The next time you kick someone's butt, ask yourself what you hoped to accomplish.
2. If your goal was to create a sense of urgency or to motivate him or her to try harder, be honest about whether it worked. If it did, great. You have done it properly.
3. If you were kicking butt because you believed that it would somehow make him or her more capable of improved performance, stop it. Find another way to coach or teach that person instead.

MAXIMIZE ENGAGEMENT AND MOTIVATION

EMPHASIZE THE WHY

We tend to focus on the *what*. What are you working on? What are your expectations? What is your plan? Most job descriptions are all about the *what*. But the *why* is also important. Understanding the *why* changes the way employees think—and feel—about their work.

Much has been written about the relationship between meaning and engagement. There is a dramatic difference in engagement between (a) employees who see their jobs merely as a set of tasks and (b) employees who perform exactly the same job, but understand the meaning of those tasks. Am I just laying bricks or am I building a school? Meaning enhances engagement.

More and more, employees want answers to the following types of questions:

1. How do I make a difference in the lives of others through my work?
2. Why is my role important to the team?
3. How does our organization contribute to a better world?

The demands of any job can create a lot of pressure to focus on the tasks at hand, to focus on the *what*. Tasks must be accomplished. Things must get done. Much of life involves unglamorously soldiering on. To increase engagement, managers must ensure that employees are aware of the *why*.

Make-A-Wish Foundation

The headquarters of the Make-A-Wish Foundation in Phoenix, Arizona, provides a terrific example of how to infuse meaning into people's work. Wherever you look, all around the office, you see images of children getting their wishes granted. Wherever you are, whatever your job, you are constantly reminded about the meaning of your work. It is very powerful.

LESSON

Day-to-day demands can cause employees to lose sight of the *why*, robbing their work of meaning. Therefore, managers should frequently remind people about the *why*.

EXPERIMENT: ARTICULATE THE *WHY*

1. Identify a role considered to be less important in your organization. This is not a high-status role.
2. For someone who works in that role, answer these questions:
   a. How do I make a difference in the lives of others through my work?
   b. Why is my role important to the team?
3. Make sure these questions are answered for employees in every role.
4. Find ways to reinforce these insights. Remind people frequently about the *why* of their jobs.
5. After 90 days, reflect on how this has made a difference for your team.

Chapter 21

MEET PEOPLE'S NEEDS

As a manager, you can create an environment that encourages people's sense of meaning in their work when you clearly articulate the why. But don't stop there. We encourage you to go several steps further. Meaningfulness and optimal engagement are highly individual, and managers have a powerful role in either maintaining (or destroying) people's sense of meaning and engagement, based on the extent to which they:[1]

- Connect work to people's personal values
- Provide recognition for a job well done
- Empower people to make the right decisions
- Build teams where supportive relationships are the norm

You support people's sense of meaningfulness and their engagement with their work when you cultivate positive relationships with them, optimize the fit between their talents and their responsibilities, and help them achieve their individual goals. When you do the opposite and fail to meet people's needs in these ways, you destroy meaning, diminish engagement, and risk losing good people. Here is an example of doing it right.

The Hotel Turnaround

Horst Schulze told me this story. Early in his career, he was given the opportunity to become the general manager of a small, poorly performing hotel in Pittsburgh, Pennsylvania. The odds of success were not good.

Upon assuming the leadership role, he called his executives together and said, "I want you to go home tonight, speak with your spouse, and decide

(continued)

(*continued*)

what is the next job you would like in this company after we succeed in turning this hotel around. Write down that career goal and bring it in tomorrow."

The next day he reviewed the goals and agreed that they were reasonable expectations. Then he said, "I make you this commitment. When we're successful in turning this hotel around, I'll do everything in my power to get each of you exactly the position you have written down."

They accomplished the turnaround and each person received the next assignment they had requested.

How do you think each of those individuals would respond if Horst called them today with a job offer? What would they say to others about working for Horst?

LESSON

The first step in engaging and motivating a particular person is to understand his or her unique configuration of needs. So what is an easy, inexpensive and effective way to understand someone's needs? *Ask them!*

You might be thinking, "That's not very profound." No, it is not. But it is not frequently and consistently practiced either. Techniques need not be profound or complicated to be effective.

EXPERIMENT: ASK THEM

1. Ask each direct report some or all of the following questions and take notes.
    a. What do you love about your work and wish you could do more of?
    b. What parts of your work are less enjoyable and you wish you could do less of?
    c. What do you love doing that is not part of your job today?
    d. Tell me about the best supervisor you ever worked for. What was there about his or her management style that worked so well for you?
    e. Tell me about some successes you have had. What was there about those situations that contributed to your ability to be successful?
    f. In what kinds of situations are you at your best?

g. What do you need from me to be at your best?
h. What do you need from your coworkers/team members to be at your best?
i. What are your career goals?
j. Tell me about the most powerful gesture of recognition you have ever received. Why was that recognition so meaningful to you?
2. As you ask your people some or all of these questions, use this information to tailor your approach to respond to each person's individual needs. In your routine interactions, you should make it a point to expand and clarify your understanding of these needs.

Once you know something about each person's needs, you must ask yourself the following two questions:

1. Can I meet those needs?
2. Do I want to meet those needs?

Managers often seek answers to this question:

"How can I retain and motivate employees when I can't meet their needs?"

The answer is simple. It cannot be done.

Imagine, for a moment, asking an analogous question about customers:

"How can I retain my customers when I cannot (or will not) meet their needs?"

Ludicrous, no? Employees, like customers, will stay only as long as their needs are being met.

LESSON

To the extent that you do not answer "Yes" to both questions (Can I meet their needs? Do I want to meet their needs?), you are reducing the likelihood that you can retain people and motivate them to perform with excellence.

Here is an example of what happens when your answer is "No."

The "Win Back" Genius

Doug Rath, cofounder of Talent Plus, and I were teaching a group of managers and executives at a long-distance telephone company. One

(continued)

(*continued*)

of these managers was the leader of the "Win Back" department. This company was losing customers at such an incredible rate they had a group of telephone salespeople whose entire mission was to call former customers and try to win them back. Each telemarketer's goal was to win back 20 customers per week in 40 hours.

They had a woman on this team who was a single mother with three children. Because of daycare challenges and related matters, she could only work three days a week. In those three days, she would routinely win back 100 customers. Routinely. Her average productivity was five times the goal in 60 percent of the time.

She came to her supervisor one day and said, "I've lost my childcare provider and I'm having a real problem finding a substitute. That means that I can't keep a regular work schedule right now until I get this figured out." She continued, "I'll give you three days a week, but I don't know what three days they are going be, and I don't know what shift, but I guarantee you I'll give you three days." Then, to the supervisor's surprise, she added, "By the way, I want a raise. I want to make what the other people make in 40 hours. I still want to work only three days a week, but I want to make the pay that other people are making in 40 hours a week."

Her supervisor consulted with his associates and got back to her with the following response. "We can't establish a precedent in which employees tell us what schedule they work. And we are not prepared to pay you for five days of work when you only work three days."

She resigned.

The seminar participants asked for our recommendations. I said, "Are you people nuts? You should call her back and say, "Listen, work whenever you want, and we are thrilled to pay you for 40 hours a week." She was five times as productive as the other employees and she was only asking for the same pay as they were receiving. She would have been a bargain at twice the price!

No matter how much that supervisor may have wanted to meet the Win Back Genius's needs, their bureaucratic organization did not allow it. The company lost 100 sales per week. How much do you think that single instance of turnover cost the company on an annual basis? This story is a great example of how the rules sometimes make it easier to fire people and harder to retain top performers.

At this point in your career, you might have your hands tied by a similar bureaucracy. But at some point, you will be the person who makes these kinds of rules. When you are in that position, remember this story.

Employees are not the only ones who need to get their needs met at work. As a manager, you have needs, too. Among other things, you need your employees to perform with excellence. Once you understand their needs, you are in a position to make a deal. "If you meet my needs for excellent performance, I'll meet yours."

The Bellman Becomes a Great Employee

Early in my career, I was the director of human resources for a large hotel with a very strong union. We had a bellman named Frank who was a borderline employee. He was very street smart. He did just enough to get by most of the time and often found ways to avoid doing even the minimum required amount of work. He received so many disciplinary memos that we had to create a second file just to contain them! Frank was good at playing this game. The union was always able to prevent us from firing him.

One day, Frank asked me for a meeting. I anticipated that he wanted to file a grievance. To my surprise, Frank said, "Mr. Sternberg, I just became engaged to be married. I came here to see what can be done about all those disciplinary memos in my file. I know I haven't been a good employee, and until now I didn't really care. But now that I'm going to have a family I need to become serious about my career. This will surprise you, but I really like this business and I would like to make a career in this company, but I know those memos will prevent me from making progress. Is there anything we can do about that?"

I heard a need. I saw an opportunity to motivate Frank. I had a need, too. Good job performance.

In essence, I had to decide whether I could meet Frank's need and whether I wanted to meet Frank's need. On the issue of can, company policy said disciplinary memos were a permanent part of the file. But I was the custodian of those records, and I had some discretion in that regard. On the issue of want, I did not particularly like Frank, but I was willing to consider meeting his need on this issue if his job performance improved. So here's what I did.

I said, "Frank, I'll make you a deal. If you can go six months without a disciplinary memo, I'll remove all those memos from your file and give you a fresh start."

Almost overnight, Frank became one of the most hardworking bellmen on our staff, and his performance remained excellent. He was meeting my needs. After six months, I fulfilled my commitment to meet his needs and removed the memos from the file. I physically handed him the memos and suggested he have a bonfire.

LESSON

Once you understand a person's needs, you are in a position to make a deal. "If you meet my needs for excellent performance, I'll meet yours."

I am not suggesting that you must meet every employee's needs. There are often situations in which your business does not enable you to meet someone's needs. Or even if you could meet them, you do not wish to do so. But don't fool yourself. If you cannot or will not meet people's needs, you diminish your ability to retain them.

Think about yourself for a moment. Recall the time that you joined your current organization. Why did you join? Be honest with yourself. For the vast majority of readers, you joined your current organization because you believed that you would get more of your needs met. See how powerful this principle is?

EXPERIMENT: MEET PEOPLE'S NEEDS

1. Begin with your top performer and answer these questions.
   a. What are that person's needs?
   b. Can I meet those needs?
   c. Do I want to meet those needs?
2. Repeat this sequence for all of your direct reports.

If you can answer the first question accurately and if you answer yes to the second and third, you will be known for your ability to retain and motivate employees.

But what can be done in situations in which you cannot meet someone's needs? There will inevitably be circumstances in which no matter how much you want to meet people's needs, you will be unable to do so. In these situations, the best you can do is demonstrate that you care, that you want to meet those needs even if you are incapable of doing so. If you are doing everything in your power to meet their needs, your employees will know it and appreciate it. But it is still no substitute for meeting their needs, and you will still be at risk of losing a good person. That is reality.

Chapter 22

DON'T SIT ON GOOD PEOPLE

As a manager, you may find it most difficult to meet people's needs when doing so could have a significant negative impact on you. Here is an example of what that might sound like: "I know he wants a promotion, but he's doing such a great job where he is, I need him to stay in that role." Whether you have said it yourself or heard another manager voice it, this kind of attitude and action from a manager has the potential to kill engagement in the people you want to retain most, your best and brightest. Here is a cautionary tale:

A Successful Manager Leaves

A restaurant manager who worked for one of my clients ran the number one restaurant in the company, according to both objective metrics (including guest and employee satisfaction scores) and subjective evaluations from executives. This restaurant was number one for four years in a row, and Verna was the manager all four years.

She clearly stated to her supervisor and to her supervisor's boss that she would like expanded responsibilities—specifically, a multidepartment leadership role. In her company, that would constitute a promotion. She had the skills, knowledge, and talent necessary to take on those responsibilities, and she knew it. Furthermore, she developed an individual who was ready to lead her department when she (the manager) left.

(continued)

(continued)

The executives in her company chose not to give Verna the promotion. They were worried that if they transferred her, the department's performance would suffer. They even increased her compensation to try to retain her.

She found a job at a competing hotel.

LESSON

When a qualified person wants a promotion or transfer, keeping that person in the current role is not a realistic option. *Your real choice is between promoting that person or losing that person from the company.* You can't tell an employee what his or her needs *ought* to be.

If you are currently doing this to someone, ask yourself this question: "If that person were taken out of that role tomorrow (for whatever reason) would we throw up our hands and declare that we can no longer function as a department?" Of course not. You and your team would figure something out. This demonstrates that if you were sufficiently motivated, you could function without that person. The employee knows this. She knows that if you cared enough, you could give her that transfer or promotion.

Perhaps this has happened (or is happening) to you. How did it feel? Did you feel like you were being punished for great performance? What did it do for your morale and engagement?

You might say, "Right now, I really do not have a viable replacement for this person." Okay, that is a common situation. But instead of merely allowing the situation to continue, make a plan. Show this person the light at the end of the tunnel. Show that you are willing to deal with the inconvenience (to you!) associated with supporting her career advancement.

Be aware that other employees are paying close attention to your actions. Whatever you choose to do, you are sending the message that this is the kind of support they will get when they are ready to move on.

If you hold people back, high-potential people will avoid your team. If you earn a reputation for helping people grow and progress in their careers, you will attract more high-potential people.

EXPERIMENT: MAKE A PLAN

1. Identify an employee who wants a transfer or promotion *and* is ready for it.
2. Make a plan to help him or her achieve career advancement in a way that minimizes the inconvenience to your department.
3. This is a long-term experiment. If you continue to do this, you will notice that top performers want to report to you, and you will be able to build a better team.

RESIST THE TEMPTATION TO SEIZE CONTROL

In the luxury hotel business, labor is the biggest controllable cost, and managers are directly responsible for it. Getting the work schedule right is important and challenging. Schedule too many employees and your payroll is too high. Schedule too few employees and the quality of service suffers. Here is a story about an all-too-common response managers make when things go awry in important areas of the business, like scheduling:

The Botched Schedule

A hotel restaurant manager really botched the employee schedule, resulting in a lot of service defects, upset guests, upset employees, and unnecessary costs (due to rework and service recovery). The general manager chewed out the food and beverage director who in turn chewed out the restaurant manager. Also, to prevent that from happening again, the food and beverage director declared that henceforth he would review all schedules from all food and beverage departments before they became final.

Have you witnessed this type of over-response before? This solution created a lot of extra work for the food and beverage director. He did not start reviewing schedules made by just that single restaurant manager. He started doing it for all the managers of all the food and beverage outlets in the hotel. It slowed things down considerably, and it sent a clear message that the department heads were no longer trusted to make proper schedules. They were closest to the needs of the business, and most of them had been exercising excellent judgment in scheduling in the outlets they managed. What do you think questioning and overriding their good judgment did to their sense of meaning and engagement with their work?

Way too often, a supervisor responds to a mistake by exercising more control, thus moving in the direction of micromanagement. Resist the temptation to do this because if you give in to it, you will eventually become overwhelmed in your efforts to control everything—and mistakes will occur anyway.

People make mistakes. That does not mean that we should be complacent, but implementing additional control mechanisms is rarely the best answer. Take your emotion out of the equation. Do not implement a cure that is worse than the disease.

In this illustration, the food and beverage director needs to address a real problem. What would be a better alternative? How could one-on-one coaching with the one hotel restaurant manager who had a problem with scheduling create a better result—for that person and for the team as a whole? What lessons and experiments from previous chapters could have helped him address this issue differently?

LESSON

Additional control mechanisms drive up costs and slow things down. If things are done right in the first place, control mechanisms add no value. When you are thinking about implementing a new control mechanism in response to a mistake, consider the costs as well as the benefits. Also consider alternative, individualized approaches that could get you even better results in the long term.

EXPERIMENT: COST/BENEFIT OF ADDITIONAL CONTROLS

The next time you are considering additional controls in response to a mistake, answer the following questions.

1. What problem are you trying to solve?
2. How frequently does it occur?
3. Estimate the costs, including nonmonetary costs. Include direct cash costs, rework, customer dissatisfaction, and others. If we assume that these costs will be eliminated, this estimate becomes the benefit of implementing the new controls.

4. In a similar way, estimate the monetary and nonmonetary costs of implementing the controls you envision.
5. Based on your answers to those questions, decide whether the new controls will really be worth the effort.
6. Consider alternative, individualized approaches to solving the problem.

Control mechanisms and oversight processes are disempowering. The next chapter explores benefits of empowering your employees, and it includes additional thoughts about control mechanisms.

Chapter 24

EMPOWER YOUR PEOPLE

L et me get my supervisor." As a customer, how many times have you heard that statement when you expressed dissatisfaction with a product or service? Or perhaps you have heard it when you requested an exception to stated procedures. As your complaint or request escalates to someone who has the authority to make a decision, you talk to the next person (and the next). How many times do you repeat your story? And how much more dissatisfied do you become with each repetition? Lack of empowerment results in terrible customer service, and, as we have suggested in previous chapters, it has a considerable negative impact on engagement, motivation, and retention.

WHO GETS TO DECIDE WHAT?

In this chapter, we focus on the following aspect of empowerment: giving employees the authority to make decisions and take action without first getting approval. Empowerment is always a matter of degree. Every employee is empowered to make some decisions without seeking approval.

LESSON

The more decisions employees are empowered to make, the higher their level of job satisfaction, the greater their degree of engagement, the more they learn, and the greater the likelihood of retaining them.

Additional benefits include improved customer service and satisfaction, increased flexibility, accelerated process improvement, and improved ability to respond to unanticipated events.

In terms of the impact on engagement and retention, the importance of empowering people cannot be over-emphasized. Empowerment contributes to psychological ownership of one's job. So why would managers not strive to give people as much empowerment as possible? Many of the reasons may sound different on the surface:

1. Managers do not want to give up control because they are accountable for the results.
2. They do not trust their employees' judgment, or they do not believe the employees have the necessary knowledge, experience, or information to make the decision.
3. They are concerned that the employees will commit malfeasance.

Though they sound different, all of those reasons boil down to one fundamental issue: lack of trust.

I wish I could remember where I picked up the following insight, but I just love it.

"In any hierarchical organization, incompetence seems to start just below wherever I am on the organization chart."

People almost never say it so blatantly, but that is a very common attitude. Many managers feel they need to control as much as they can because they do not fully trust "those people down there."

"But," you say, "I don't want to control everything, I just want sign off on it so I know what's going on." That is a copout. You can know what is going on if you are informed after the fact. The requirement to sign off before implementation exists so you can maintain the power to veto it. Here is a story to illustrate this from a seminar participant named Charlie:

The Chief Steward Proves a Point

Charlie was chief steward in a very large, luxury hotel. The chief steward is responsible for the crew that washes and manages all the china, glass, flatware, pots, pans, and kitchen equipment—among many other important duties.

"When I need to order cleaning chemicals," Charlie said, "I need four signatures: the food and beverage director, the director of purchasing, the controller, and the general manager. One day, I asked the general manager why we needed all those signatures because they slowed the process. He told me that we needed standard controls over all purchasing decisions. I replied that I was the only person who had the information to know how much we needed to order, but he would not consider changing the process. So the next week, when I had to order cleaning chemicals, I wrote a purchase order for *100 times* the amount of chemicals I actually needed. This would have cost a lot of extra money. *They all signed the P.O.!*"

Charlie's next move took enviable courage. He took the signed P.O. to the general manager and asked, "Where is the control? You all signed this because you trust me."

What value did the signatures add? Maybe there is a need to have more than one signature to prevent collusion (lack of trust, again, by the way). But four signatures? How do you think Charlie felt? Like a trusted, respected staff member or more like a peon whose judgment and ethics could not be trusted? Charlie's story demonstrates that all the people whose signatures he needed saw Charlie as trustworthy. They accepted his order without questioning it. But the process they had created added no value, did not accomplish its purported purpose, and wasted productive time.

You might advance all kinds of good reasons for all those signatures, but be clear and honest about the impact of this process on engagement and retention. And don't kid yourself about the culture such a process creates.

The Twenty-Five Dollar Decision

In the luxury hotel business, sales reps routinely send guests amenities such as flowers or wine, or a nice fruit and cheese plate. Bruce, a sales rep for a hotel, told me that he needed three signatures every time he wanted to send one of these amenities: the director of sales, the controller, and the general manager. The way the business works, the decision to send these types of amenities is often last minute. Consequently, he had to walk the form around to get the necessary signatures. Typically, the cost of each amenity was about $25. He and his fellow sales reps were entrusted to bring in the vast majority of the hotel's revenue, but they were not empowered to make a $25 *decision!*

You might say that it is not a matter of trust, and you might give him all the business reasons you want about why this must be the process, but without a doubt the message Bruce hears is, "We do not trust you to make a $25 decision." Bruce hears this message because, despite all the spin you might apply, the fundamental reason is lack of trust.

That policy diminished the sales reps' job satisfaction, engagement, and motivation. We had it changed, by the way, after we computed that the policy cost the hotel more than 600 hours of productive selling time per year for the whole department, because of the time required to get the necessary signatures.

The previous stories have focused on what happens (and how it feels) when you disempower people. Here is an example of what can happen when you truly empower people. Among other things, this story illustrates the dramatic shift in attitude, performance, and culture when you do give people the authority to make important decisions.

Hourly Employees to Do Their Own Hiring

When I was general manager of The Ritz-Carlton, Tysons Corner, my executives and I decided to empower the hourly employees to do the hiring for new hourly employees in the hotel. Before that, we used a standard hiring process in which human resources conducted a thorough screening interview and then referred finalists to the department manager for the final interview and decision. The department manager would extend offers to successful candidates pending references.

Our new process did not include anyone in supervision or management. Human resources would perform a three-minute screen to ensure that the candidate met some very basic requirements such as availability for the required shifts, being old enough to serve alcohol (depending on the job), or similar necessary qualifications. Human resources would then refer candidates to a select group of hourly employees in the appropriate department who performed the final interviews.

We were, at the time, working with Talent Plus®, an international human resources consulting firm based in Lincoln, Nebraska. (Larry and Kim have both been employed by Talent Plus since the late 1990s). Talent Plus trained these employees to interview and evaluate candidates using a scientifically validated structured interview. Nobody in human resources or management interviewed candidates for hourly jobs.

The hourly interviewers referred successful candidates to a panel of several other hourly employees in the appropriate department. If this panel endorsed the candidate, the hourly employees made job offers (we gave them a "fill-in-the-blanks" script) and checked references. They then informed human resources about who had been hired and when they would report to work.

You may be thinking, "That simply can't be true. Nobody would do that. Larry is exaggerating." But it's true. We did that, and I'm not exaggerating. The process was remarkably effective.

I am not telling the story to persuade you to try this. I am telling the story to help you understand the striking change in attitude and performance that occurred as a result of this level of empowerment. Compare the traditional approach to the empowered approach.

Here is the former, more traditional situation. You and I work in department X. We have a very demanding, busy week coming up and our team is short two hourly employees. Human resources and the department manager are accountable to fill these jobs, but they have not done so. Because they did not do their jobs, we are going to have to do extra work this coming week, while the company saves the expense of the two employees. The job satisfaction on our team is not enhanced by this situation because we are smart enough to know that the manager will look better because of the reduced payroll costs. The motivational speech the manager gives about producing excellence under adversity rings a little hollow.

Maybe the manager is worried about getting through the week short-staffed, so he or she compromises the hiring standards and hires two warm bodies. Now we are stuck having to work with these unsatisfactory performers—and not just for this week, either. Our manager did this to us. This does not enhance our engagement or our job satisfaction. It does not contribute to our retention.

Does any of this sound familiar to you? Have you seen this movie before?

Now, contrast the traditional approach with what happens when the employees are empowered to make their own hiring decisions. Our hourly interviewers have been interviewing but they have not found anybody good enough to join our team. They say to the rest us, "Look, we could hire a couple of the people we've interviewed but we honestly do not think they're good enough for our team." Our team then decides to get through the week short-staffed, but it is our decision. Our attitude about the week is entirely different. We motivate each other to produce excellence. Our relationships are deepened as we live out our decision to face this adversity together.

Or we choose the alternative. We hire a couple of warm bodies, fully conscious that we are compromising to get through the week. We are still stuck with these people after the week is over. But we have nobody to blame but ourselves. It is not management's fault. And we know we can make a different decision the next time this situation occurs.

Here is an important side note to this story. As it happens, the Talent Plus structured interview returns a score for each candidate. This score indicates the candidate's overall aptitude to perform the job with excellence. The higher the score, the more talented the candidate. Because management had been using the same interview to evaluate candidates, we decided to compare the scores of the people hired by the managers to the scores of the people hired by the hourly employees. The employees had higher standards than the managers. They had to work shoulder to shoulder with these people every day. They did not want the hassles of working with unsatisfactory performers.

Workers who decide how to get their work done (empowerment) enjoy a high degree of engagement. In the best cases, this includes deciding how to redesign processes and procedures.

Motivating People to Give Suggestions

I remember being at The Ritz-Carlton corporate office when there were several gentlemen conducting a benchmarking visit. The vice president of quality asked me to join one of their meetings. Here was the question they were asking: "How do you motivate people to give suggestions for improvement?"

They were brainstorming ways to motivate people to give suggestions, and uncharacteristically I was sitting there with my mouth shut listening to this conversation, which, frankly, I thought was ridiculous. The vice president of quality invited me to contribute my thoughts, which constitutes a lesson this chapter:

LESSON

You do not need to motivate people to give suggestions for improvement. You just need to quit discouraging them or punishing them for giving suggestions.

People are full of suggestions; they have plenty of ideas. Tragically, many companies and cultures systematically demotivate people from giving suggestions.

A very common situation occurs when an employee makes a suggestion to his or her manager to change one of their processes. It is not unusual for a manager to listen to the suggestion and reply, "I can understand why you might think that would work, but I have 15 years of experience in this, and I've tried that before twice. It doesn't work." Sound familiar? They do not try the suggestion. Nobody learns anything.

And how motivated do you think that employee is to submit the next suggestion?

Consider a team of empowered employees who have the authority to redesign how they get their work done. In this scenario, the employee team has 51 percent of the vote about their processes. Now they come to the manager with the same suggestion. But now they are seeking advice rather than approval. The manager gives the same response: "I can understand why you might think that would work, but I have 15 years of experience in this, and I've tried that before twice. It doesn't work." But the employees are not persuaded. They are empowered to decide, and they do decide to try the new approach.

If it works, both the manager and the employees have learned something. If it does not work, the employees have learned that the manager's advice is worth more consideration than they gave it. They might well give the manager's advice more weight in the future.

LESSON

When people are more empowered, more learning occurs, whether their suggestions work or not.

Furthermore, if a suggestion works, the employees experience the kind of self-actualization that is usually available only to managers. They get to come to work every day and say to themselves, "I did that. I created that success." And it *is* their success. They will be highly motivated to create the next improvement. In fact, in those situations, the manager can dial up this motivation by setting the right expectation, in the right way for future decisions, "Wow! You people are terrific. I can't wait to see what you do next!"

You may be asking, "But what do you do if it does not work? Yes, they have learned something, but now you have a bad process. If they have 51 percent of the vote, what do you do?"

That is a terrific question. The short answer is: Change it. Isn't this what you should do when a manager tries a new process that does not work?

Empowerment works in your favor here, too. When the empowered employees have tried a new process (their process) that does not work, they will often decide to change it, even before the manager has the opportunity to discuss it with them. Who wants ineffective processes? Certainly not the people who have to use them. This is what people will do in a culture that fosters empowerment and psychological ownership.

This discussion provides another powerful illustration of the difference in attitude and performance when you give people more power. By contrast, think about a less empowered model. A manager decides to change a process. He or she gets some input from the employees, but, ultimately, the manager redesigns the process. He or she explains why to the employees and trains them on the new process. As in the preceding discussion, either it works or it does not work.

If it works, everybody is better off and they appreciate it. Learning occurs for everyone. But the self-actualization belongs to the manager. The employees have no psychological ownership. This is not bad. But it could be better.

The most important difference is observed when it does not work. When it does not work, does the manager immediately change the process? Not a chance. The manager says, "I know this will work. The root cause of the problem is that the employees are not committed. They're not executing the process the way they're supposed to."

The next thing you know, the manager is retraining everyone and reexplaining why this new process will make things better. What do the employees hear? "It's your fault this is not working." They hear that because they're smart and they know that is the real message, however it might be worded. This is hurting their engagement, their motivation, and their likelihood of retention.

When a manager decides to try something new, in the vast majority of cases, he or she will require people to keep trying for a much longer period of time than when the employees own the decision.

LESSON

Empowerment accelerates change.

As you can plainly see, in this discussion about empowerment we are talking not merely about allowing people to give their input about decisions; we are talking about a genuine transfer of power. This transfer can be scary because you cannot divest yourself of accountability. As a result, many managers take the position, "If I'm accountable, I need to make the decisions." We understand that point of view. Many managers are not interested in taking the risks associated with a high degree of empowerment.

Implementing this approach requires a great deal of respect and trust in employees at every level: respect for their intelligence and trust in their motives. It requires you as the manager to acknowledge that you do not know everything, and that people with less education and less experience might well have a better idea. It requires you to abandon the (often unconscious) attitude that "those people" can't be trusted to make good decisions.

Getting started, however, is easy if you are willing to try an experiment.

EXPERIMENT: INCREASE EMPOWERMENT

1. Ask your people this question: What decisions do you need approval for that you are fully competent to make today?
2. If someone needs some education, training, or coaching before you are willing to empower them, provide it.
3. Give people as much decision-making authority as you can. Take some risks.
4. Celebrate successes. Do not punish failures.
5. Review both successes and failures to see what you can learn.

Have a bias in favor of letting people try things, even if you think they probably will not work. Look for opportunities to let your people make decisions. Trust that they will change things that do not work. Remember:

LESSON

The more decisions an employee is empowered to make, the higher the level of job satisfaction, the greater the degree of engagement, the more the person learns, and the greater the likelihood of retention.

HARNESS DISCRETIONARY EFFORT

Discretionary effort is not a new idea. The value of "going the extra mile" goes back to the Roman Empire and the Sermon on the Mount. In that time and place, Roman soldiers could order anyone living under Roman martial law to carry their gear for a mile (and not a step farther). In the Sermon on the Mount, Jesus urged his followers, "If a soldier demands that you carry his gear for a mile, carry it two miles" (Matthew 5:41, NLT), and the idea of going the extra mile was born. The fact that it has been around so long should tell us something. Discretionary effort is the level of effort one is capable of giving to a task, assignment, or mission above and beyond the minimum required, and it can have an impressive impact on outcomes. Here is an example.

Cindi Sets the Standard

Our former associate, Cindi, created the warm welcome experience for visitors to our company's headquarters. This included people who called on the phone as well as those who visited in person. Coincidentally, our phone number was very similar to the phone number of a local hospital, which resulted in frequent wrong numbers.

Cindi knew that people attempting to call the hospital were often anxious and stressed. She could have just said, very pleasantly, "I'm sorry, you've called the wrong number." But she did not do that.

(continued)

(*continued*)

She could have given them the hospital's number. But she did not do that, either.

Cindi *transferred* them to the hospital. That is discretionary effort at its finest, and it represented our brand exquisitely.

This is another favorite discretionary effort story:

The Engineer and the Video Tape

A famous speaker was hired to deliver a keynote address at a major conference being held at a Ritz-Carlton Hotel. A certain video was an important part of the keynote. This was long before digital recording. The video was on a magnetic tape. Somehow, the night before the keynote someone spilled Coke on the tape, rendering it useless. There was no way to replace the tape or get another copy in time.

Without being asked, an engineer decided to clean the tape. He went into an unoccupied function room and set numerous six-foot, schoolroom type tables end to end. He unwound the videotape onto those tables. Then he took methyl alcohol and cotton swabs and he cleaned the entire tape on both sides, inch by inch. It took hours. It worked perfectly the next morning.

That speaker sang his praises (and the praises of the hotel) all over the country, long after the conference had come and gone.

LESSON

All people have a considerable reservoir of discretionary effort at their disposal every day. Tapping it simultaneously improves quality, productivity, and job satisfaction.

As a manager, how do you tap it? There are no silver bullets, but here are a few things to think about.

1. Explicitly state that making a difference is one of your values. Publicize stories like Cindi's to provide vivid examples of what that means. Then continuously challenge every employee to find ways to make a difference.

2. Clearly articulate your organization's mission in the world so employees know that they are part of something bigger than themselves. Make sure they know how their specific efforts further that mission. This adds meaningfulness to their work.

3. Help people understand that going the extra mile involves little additional time and work. Very often, a small bit of extra effort makes a huge difference.

4. Be a role model and go the extra mile yourself. Do not be content with "good enough." Demand excellence from yourself and from others. Excellence requires discretionary effort.

5. Select for your team people who have a burning desire to excel and who are "hardwired" to put forth the extra effort necessary for extraordinary performance.

That last point cannot be over-emphasized. If you select people who just want to get by, then no mission and no combination of positive and negative consequences will get you there. You must have people who want it, and want it in their bones.

EXPERIMENT: COLLECT AND DISTRIBUTE STORIES OF DISCRETIONARY EFFORT

1. Over the next week, pay attention to instances in which an employee has really gone above and beyond. Solicit stories from your employees.

2. Preserve the story. Write it down, make a video, whatever has to be done.

3. Celebrate the employees who demonstrate this kind of discretionary effort.

4. Find ways to disseminate those stories as examples of the kind of effort your organization values.

5. Over time, see if this practice generates more discretionary effort.

SOLICIT VOLUNTEERS FOR UNPOPULAR TASKS

A management seminar participant said there were tasks in his department that nobody wanted to do. "What," he asked, "do you do with those?" The reaction of his fellow participants was immediate and surprisingly consistent. Almost all of them were in the same situation, and almost all were dissatisfied with the obvious solutions, which include:

1. Saying to the employee, "I know it is not your favorite thing, but it is part of your job. Every job has things you would rather not do."
2. Rotating the undesired tasks among the team members, thus equitably distributing the burden.
3. Including the boss in the rotation.
4. Drawing straws.
5. Paying an incentive for those tasks.

Nobody reported great success with these solutions. However, there were a couple of participants who had discovered an alternative approach. The first was a controller, whose broad responsibilities included both accounting and nonaccounting functions. There were several tasks widely considered undesirable by his staff. One day, out of the blue, he got the idea to make a list of all tasks for which his team was responsible. He posted the list and asked his people to sign their names by the tasks they most liked to do. That was his solution.

He was shocked that even the undesirable tasks had names by them. He mentioned in particular the task of wrapping packages. He was absolutely certain that nobody liked doing that. But there were two employees who were really good at it and really enjoyed it, and they signed up to do it.

Thereafter, he abandoned the notion of equally distributing tasks in favor of what we might now call job sculpting—assigning responsibilities based on what each person likes to do and is good at.

Another participant was the manager of a fast food restaurant. The unpleasant task in that business was cleaning bathrooms. Coincidentally, he used the same approach and experienced the same results. When he posted the list, he discovered a couple of employees who liked to clean and who realized that clean bathrooms gave the restaurant a strong competitive advantage. They understood the "why" of the task. As you can imagine, these employees were regularly celebrated by their associates who were relieved of this duty.

Can it really be that simple? Sometimes it is. Give it a try. What have you got to lose?

LESSON

Even unpopular tasks might have some takers if you just ask.

EXPERIMENT: ASK FOR VOLUNTEERS

1. Before you assign tasks to specific team members, ask them to identify the tasks they would most like to do.
2. If certain people sign up for tasks that others would rather avoid, create a plan that enables those doing the unpopular tasks to be relieved of other duties so that they can spend more time on those tasks. In other words, the plan should not require them to carry more than their fair share.
3. See what this does for engagement and motivation in your department.

CREATE A SENSE OF URGENCY

Creating a sense of urgency is about motivating people to take immediate, earnest action.

The fact is that most employees are taking immediate action on something. They are pursuing some things with a sense of urgency. For most employees, your challenge is not to create a sense of urgency. The challenge is to motivate employees to demonstrate a sense of urgency about the things you care about.

A mentor, Sigi Brauer, gave this excellent advice: "Make your boss's priorities your own." Setting direction and articulating the values of the organization are two of the most important things a manager can do. If you have not clearly articulated your goals and values, how do employees know where to focus their energy? How can they know what to have a sense of urgency about?

Even if you have clearly articulated your goals and values, immediate priorities shift continuously. In the luxury hotel business, there are daily meetings throughout the hotel to inform employees about the current situation and matters of greatest urgency. For example, is the plumbing broken? What VIPs are arriving? Is the union about to call a strike? Are labor costs too high? There is always something about which employees should have a sense of urgency.

Absent real-time information about the immediate challenges faced by your organization, how can employees possibly know how to focus their sense of urgency?

LESSON

As a manager, you have information that is otherwise unavailable to employees, and you have a perspective about the big picture that they can't possibly have. Absent that perspective, they might not recognize the importance of an event. You must help employees understand what is going on and what it means to your organization. Then you can call them to action. You can ask for a sense of urgency and you will get it.

One final point. Many employees (and managers!) are burdened by too many "number one" priorities, about which they are expected to demonstrate a sense of urgency. If everything is a "number one" priority, nothing is. This situation decreases their sense of urgency because they know they cannot meet the expectations. They disengage. Don't create this scenario for employees.

EXPERIMENT: CREATE A SENSE OF URGENCY

1. Ask your employees what they think is their number one priority today.
2. See if they are giving you the right answer.
3. If yes, good for you.
4. If no, make a correction. Explain why.
5. Repeat this as often as necessary until your employees are in sync with you.

SET CHALLENGING GOALS

Numerous highly respected authorities give the following advice: "When setting goals with your employees, make sure those goals are reasonable and attainable. Otherwise you will demotivate your employees." But what about dreaming big? What about Big Hairy Audacious Goals (BHAGs)? What looks impossible to one person might look intriguing to another.

People can easily have conflicting points of view about what is reasonable. But Dr. Fred Jervis taught his students and mentees another way to think about goals. He taught us to visualize ideal outcomes (not reasonable ones) and then ask the question, "If we want to achieve that, how would we do it?"

The Jervis question is scary. It demands the courage to try new strategies. It takes us into uncharted territory.

The San Francisco Hotel Union

When I was vice president of human resources for the Portman Hotel Company, we were opening a hotel in San Francisco, a city with a very strong hotel union. The owner of the hotel directed us to open and operate a union-free hotel. This was not a reasonable goal. We asked the Jervis question, "If we want to open and operate union-free, how will we do it?" In brainstorming possible answers to that question, we came up with several nonstandard strategies. The most radical was: Give employees a contract, just like they would get with a union. The contract we gave them included strong, legally binding commitments including wage increases and the right to arbitrate grievances. We opened that hotel union-free, and it stayed that way.

LESSON

Set ideal goals, even if they might seem unreasonable on their face. Reasonable goals do not fully engage top performers. Top performers get excited about audacious goals that require creativity, determination, and extraordinary performance. High-potential employees want a manager who will inspire them to ideal, exceptional accomplishments.

We anticipate a large number of, "Yeah but . . ." reactions to this point of view. After all, numerous authorities disagree with it. But think about yourself for a second. How excited do you get about "reasonable" goals? How much discretionary effort are they likely to inspire in you? How much more engaged and energized do you get when you have to be creative because tried and true methods will not suffice? Do you find audacious goals more stimulating and potentially meaningful than reasonable ones?

Even if your organization holds you accountable to achieve a set of reasonable goals, you can still do this experiment. It is definitely not for everybody. But if this calls to you, it'll be a lot of fun.

EXPERIMENT: VISUALIZE IDEAL GOALS

Brainstorm the answer to these questions:

1. If our team had a truly remarkable year, what would we accomplish? What outcomes would really make us proud?
2. If we achieve those outcomes, how will we know it?
3. What can we do differently to achieve those outcomes?
4. Implement one or two items from the list generated for the preceding question.
5. After 90 days, reflect on your experience. How has this approach affected your team's performance?

Even if you do not fully achieve your audacious goal, you will almost certainly accomplish more than if you had set a reasonable goal.

BE UNREASONABLY OPTIMISTIC

I f you are going to set audacious (possibly unreasonable) goals, you will need a high level of optimism (possibly unreasonable optimism) to keep you on the path to achieving them. Here is a great story of how unreasonable optimism can work in your favor.

The Unmovable Float

My former boss and mentor, Sigi Brauer, was relentlessly positive and unfailingly optimistic. One spring weekend, I was one of several people visiting his home on Lake Winnipesaukee in New Hampshire. His lakefront amenities included a floating platform you could swim to from the shore. Because the lake iced over during the winter, the platform had been pulled onto the shore, which consisted entirely of large boulders. So at the time of my visit, the platform was out of the water, sitting on the boulders.

It was late spring. The ice had melted, and the water temperature was rising. It was just barely warm enough to swim. Because two of the visitors were adult males, Sigi invited us to help put the float back into the water. We marched down the slope to the platform. It was a large wooden platform sitting atop several full-sized metal garbage cans—a very heavy object, indeed. We did our best to move it. We tried each person taking a different corner. We tried all three of us on one corner. We tried all kinds of variations. The platform did not budge, even a bit.

(continued)

(*continued*)

It was obvious to me that we were not going to move that platform. I would have accepted reality and given up. But Sigi remained—quite unreasonably—optimistic that we would figure out a solution. He insisted that we keep trying. So we did, to no avail. However, while we were futilely trying to move this thing, a completely unanticipated solution appeared.

Two young men in their early twenties cruised by in a boat. They were just cruising around, drinking beer, and hanging out. They saw what we were trying to do, stopped their boat, and swam over to help us. With five guys, it was easy. In a few minutes, we moved that baby into the water. No problem.

We were lucky they came by. However, without Sigi's unreasonable optimism, we would not have been there to solicit the help. We would have failed.

LESSON

Optimism empowers people to move into challenging situations. It fosters persistence in the face of setbacks. It improves creativity and resourcefulness, and it results in better problem solving.

Optimism is contagious. And so is lack of optimism. What are your people catching from you?

BUILD EXTRAORDINARY TEAMS

RECRUIT CONTINUOUSLY

C ontinuous recruiting is the foundation for building extraordinary teams. In many organizations, the human resources department bears the primary responsibility for recruiting. This leads many managers down the wrong path, and they do not take any responsibility for recruiting. No matter how great your human resources department may be, do not make the mistake of leaving your fate entirely in their hands. Recruit continuously, looking for the right people for your team, and send HR good candidates you have already identified and vetted.

Be proactive. Be the kind of manager who is constantly looking for talented people, even if you do not have an opening. Because so many organizations run quite lean with their staffing, when someone leaves, the pressure to fill the position tempts managers and human resources departments to compromise their hiring standards rather than hold out for the right person. If you have been proactively recruiting, you will have more (and better) options, and you will not have to compromise on talent to quickly fill a vacancy.

Create a talent bench. This is a group of external candidates who have the right talent and would be a good fit for your team, but for whom you do not have a position at the moment. To create a strong bench, you must recruit continuously, whether you have openings or not. The more candidates you have who are already qualified, the stronger your bench.

I once knew an executive chef of a very large hotel in Manhattan who made it his business to interview one sous chef candidate every week. When one of his sous chefs left, he immediately knew who he was going to call to fill that position.

LESSON

Proactivity makes a difference. If you recruit continuously, when someone leaves, you already have candidates in mind. This way, you can fill the position more rapidly without compromising the quality of your final selection.

To find the right candidates, start by asking your employees—but not all of them—for referrals. Ask your best people. It turns out that birds of a feather really do flock together. Top performers know other top performers. This only works, however, if you ask through one-on-one conversations.

Treat recruiting like brainstorming. Let ideas happen without contradiction. One of your top performers might think of someone and then immediately tell you why that person would not want to work on your team. Go ahead and contact that person anyway. Your goal is simply to get to know the person. He might not be interested today, and you do not have a position to offer today. But you might have a position next week, and he might be interested next week. He might also know someone who would be interested in future opportunities on your team. So even if he will almost certainly say, "No, thanks," contact him anyway.

LESSON

To build the strongest talent bench for your team, have one-on-one conversations with your best people and ask them for referrals. Even if the referral is likely to say, "No thanks," contact that person anyway.

When you are asking them for referrals, your top performers might need help thinking of people to recommend.

Here are some possible questions that might stimulate their thinking:

1. Who is the best [JOB TITLE] with whom you have worked?
2. Who was the best [JOB TITLE] at [THEIR FORMER PLACE OF WORK]?
3. Who are the best [JOB TITLE] in town?
4. Who do you know who is honest, hardworking, and has a great positive attitude?

EXPERIMENT: RECRUIT CONTINUOUSLY

1. Set a goal to interview at least one external candidate every week.
2. After the interview, decide whether you want to put this person on your talent bench.
3. After 90 days, how many people do you have on your talent bench?

As you add people to your talent bench, you need a systematic way to stay in touch so they know you have not forgotten them. This could be periodic emails, texts, LinkedIn messages, or even phone calls. These small gestures demonstrate to potential team members that they are significant to you. The more you individualize these communications, the more significant each person feels. When you do have an opportunity for them, they are much more likely to respond favorably.

LESSON

Stay in touch with candidates on your talent bench. These communications make them feel significant, increasing the ease of bringing them onto your team when you do have an opening.

EXPERIMENT: STAY IN TOUCH

1. Implement a plan to keep those people engaged until you have the right opportunity for them.
2. Continue this for 90 days. How many people do you have on your bench? How has it helped you when someone on your team has left?

BET ON TALENT

Continuously recruiting for your talent bench is the foundation for building extraordinary teams because extraordinary teams cannot exist without the right people. How are you defining the "right people" for your team? And what is the payoff for betting on talent? The stories and lessons of this chapter answer those questions.

LESSON

In building an extraordinary team your most important decisions involve who joins your team. In the words of legendary college basketball coach John Wooden, "Not every coach can win with talent, but no coach can win without it."

Affirmative Action Quotas

In 1979, I moved to Atlantic City, New Jersey, to begin a new job as vice president of human resources for the Playboy Hotel and Casino, which was under construction. Those were heady days in Atlantic City. Too many casinos to count were also under construction. It was a genuine boomtown. There were cranes everywhere you looked. Tens of thousands of jobs were being created. It was very exciting to be a part of it.

(continued)

(*continued*)

The State of New Jersey authorized casino gaming not only to accomplish economic goals, but also to accomplish social goals. Understandably, the state wanted to ensure that casinos would work aggressively to achieve ethnic, racial, and gender diversity among their employee populations. It might seem hard to believe now, but we had to achieve certain quotas to be granted a license to operate our casino.

One day, the gaming commission called me to ask who was going to be in charge of our affirmative action program. I told them that the assistant director of human resources would have that as one of her responsibilities. They informed me that that was unacceptable. If we wanted our license, we would have to staff a person whose only responsibility was affirmative action. All casinos had the same requirement.

All the other casinos hired experts from all over the country to head up their affirmative action programs. These experts typically possessed advanced degrees and had studied affirmative action and diversity extensively. They were honestly impressive individuals. They knew affirmative action backward and forward.

I hired a local used car salesman named Ron. He did not have an advanced degree. He had no formal expertise in affirmative action. But in addition to selling cars, Ron was a community activist and leader. He was extremely well connected in Atlantic City. He knew how to get things done in that town. He could make a few phone calls, and the right candidates would show up to fill our quotas.

Ron outperformed all those experts with all those credentials because at the end of the day, their academic knowledge did not really matter. The gaming commission was interested in only one thing: Did you fill your quotas?

How necessary are the requirements you have for various jobs on your team or in your organization? It is not unusual to see a requirement for a college degree when a degree is not really necessary to do the job with excellence. Another common but unnecessary requirement: A minimum amount of experience. However, for entry-level, rank and file jobs, experience is not that important. In fact, lack of experience is the only deficiency that corrects itself over time. If you hire someone with no experience today, two years from now, he or she will have two years of experience.

LESSON

Do not establish requirements that are not really necessary. This can cause you to screen out the best candidates.

Unnecessary requirements can also limit the diversity of your talent pool, as this next story illustrates.

The Female Doorman

The Omni International Hotel in Norfolk, Virginia, had an opening for a doorman, for which they advertised in the paper (this was before online recruiting was possible). At that time, I was the corporate director of human resources. I received a complaint from an individual who had been turned down for the job. She felt she had been the victim of illegal discrimination because she was a woman.

I immediately found her complaint to be credible. At that time, it was very unusual to see a female doorman—or door person. So there was clearly some sort of institutional bias at work, whether it was conscious or not.

In this instance, the front office manager was the hiring manager. I called him to discuss the decision. He reported that the uniforms they had would not fit her. They would all be too big (because only men had been doing that job). However, this was a luxury hotel. They had a seamstress on staff for the express purpose of making uniforms fit properly.

I said, "What else do you have?"

He replied, "The job requires the employee to lift heavy luggage out of the trunk of a car. She wouldn't be able to do that."

I am not making this next part up. I swear. I had obtained from human resources a copy of her job application. I said, "Did you look at the hobbies she listed? The first one is 'weight lifting.'" Honest to God.

He gave up, and at my direction, they hired her. On her first day of work, she garnered terrific PR for the hotel. Because a female doorperson was so rare, a reporter wrote an article about it. Her presence in that role became a unique feature of the hotel.

But how can you really know whether someone can do the job? Best practice includes scientific assessment as a step in the selection process. The following story illustrates how scientific assessment can improve both the diversity of the people you hire and the odds that they will be top performers.

The Portman Hotel

In the 1980s, John Portman, famous architect and real estate developer, decided to build a hotel in San Francisco. For marketing and branding purposes, the hotel became a member of the Peninsula Hotel Group. That membership required us to provide butler-style service to all guests. To provide that service, we need to find people who could clean a guestroom at the same level of quality as a housekeeper in a five-star hotel and who had the guest relations skills of a top-level waiter or concierge, *and* who liked to do both every day.

If you ask most hoteliers, they will tell you that the people cleaning toilets generally prefer to avoid face-to-face guest service, and the people personally serving the guests do not want to clean toilets every day. So we faced a dilemma.

Traditional approaches to recruiting and selecting employees would not find people with the particular combination of talent we needed, so I started searching for alternative methods. I found a group of people who said, "We can absolutely help you identify people like that because we measure aptitude, which is independent of experience, knowledge, and expertise. Through the use of our scientific assessments, we will tell you whether someone has the talent to do that job with excellence *and* whether they will enjoy it. You just have to be willing to give them the training and knowledge they need to succeed in the job."

After learning more about their approach, we decided to partner with this group, which at the time was known as Selection Research Incorporated. We decided that for entry-level positions and for first-line supervisors, we would not require any experience, and we would base our hiring decisions on talent as measured by their assessments.

Because experience was no longer a factor, we contacted all the organizations in San Francisco whose mission included helping their constituents find jobs. We said, "Send your people. No experience necessary." And send people they did.

We assessed about 9,500 candidates to hire 350 people for the opening of this hotel. The results were remarkable. Because we focused on talent rather than knowledge and experience, some of the most common barriers to employment disappeared. The assessment also reduced the subjectivity of the interviewers.

One of the most surprising outcomes was that the demographics of our 350-person staff was *to the percentage point* the demographics of the city of San Francisco. And, as you know, San Francisco is extremely diverse.

LESSON

You can actually expand your pool of candidates *and increase your diversity* if you get rid of unnecessary requirements.

Talent does not know race, ethnicity, gender, age, or any other category. If you focus on talent you will get a diverse workforce—and not only a diverse workforce, but also a high-performance workforce.

EXPERIMENT: IDENTIFY HIRING CRITERIA THAT REALLY MATTER

To know what a great candidate looks like for a particular job, you need to invest some time to understand what a top performer looks like in that job.

1. Think about the best performer you have ever personally worked with in that job.
2. Make a list of not more than 10 things that made that person such an outstanding performer.
3. Circle the three items that contributed most to their exemplary performance.
4. Ask a few coworkers to do this.
5. Identify the items that come up with the greatest frequency.
6. As you interview candidates, downplay experience and education, and focus on the items from the preceding step on this list. Focus on them in reference checks as well.
7. After you've hired three people using this approach, review how it has worked for you.

ENSURE THE RIGHT FIT

As we discussed in the previous chapter, to build an extraordinary team you should make sure that new hires have the talent to perform with excellence. Along with talent, however, you must also evaluate the issue of fit. As you know, organizational cultures differ, management styles differ, and business challenges differ. Remember the GIFT Formula discussion from Chapter 14:

$$(\text{Talent} + \text{Fit}) \times \text{Investment} = \text{Growth}$$

If your goal is to build extraordinary teams, and if you want to get the greatest return on your investments in your team members, you must pay attention to both talent and fit.

Chris and the Caribbean Hotel

A recruiter called me to check a reference on my friend Chris, who was being considered for a general manager role for a Caribbean hotel. I asked the recruiter to tell me more about the specific expectations and challenges of the job. He relayed that the hotel was the most prominent business on the island, and therefore the hotel's general manager would be involved with the governor and would have to be heavily involved in community affairs. As I listened, it became evident that the job involved a lot of politics. Chris was a great guy and a talented general manager, but he was a very blunt and straightforward individual. He was not a good diplomat and he was not at all good at politics.

I told the recruiter that I did not recommend Chris for the job. He was dumbfounded. "But Chris put your name as a reference," he said. "What am I going to tell him?" I said, "Don't worry, I will tell him myself. There is no way he would be happy in that job."

(continued)

(*continued*)

I immediately called Chris and explained why he should stay away from that job. Chris thanked me and withdrew as a candidate.

LESSON

A person can have plenty of talent for a job, but not be a good fit.

We Are Never Satisfied

I once worked with a highly talented chief executive officer whose motto was, "We are never satisfied." His drive for continuous improvement was relentless. I assure you, not everyone was a good fit with his style. Some really good people were exhausted by his attitude. But others saw him as a kindred spirit. So when we were selecting direct reports for him, we gave candidates this motto and paid attention to their reaction. Some asked with hope, "Is this really true?" One said, "What a sad way to be." Neither response is inherently more desirable than the other under every circumstance. But in this circumstance, it was a critical element of fit.

The experiment here is similar to the experiment in the previous chapter but the focus is on fit rather than talent for the job.

EXPERIMENT: WHAT MAKES SOMEONE A GOOD FIT FOR YOU?

1. Identify three people who thrive in your organizational culture under your unique management style.
2. For each person, identify what makes them such a good fit.
3. Ask each of those people to say what *they* think makes them a good fit.
4. Identify items that you all seem to agree on.
5. As you interview candidates, focus on the items from the preceding step.
6. After you have hired three people using this approach, review how it has worked for you.

MATCH THE RIGHT PEOPLE TO THE RIGHT TRAINING

Training is an investment managers make in their people. Many managers make the mistake of believing that, with the right training, anyone can become an expert at anything. Managers who build extraordinary teams know better. They know that investments in training make the biggest difference and yield the greatest returns when they are aimed at the right people, who have the right talents. Remember the GIFT Formula. Investment is a multiplier on the combination of talent and fit.

$$(\text{Talent} + \text{Fit}) \times \text{Investment} = \text{Growth}$$

The returns on that investment can go straight to the bottom line. The same training delivered the same way will not create the same performance in people who start off with different levels of talent. Sales results from a Talent Plus partnership with a luxury cosmetics retailer bear out that claim.

The ROI of Talent

In partnership with the retailer, Talent Plus created a pre-hire talent assessment for cosmetic sales associates. People with varying levels of talent were hired for the same type of position and received the same training. When sales performance was measured later, those with higher talent for

(continued)

141

(*continued*)

the role based on the pre-hire talent assessment outperformed their less talented peers.

Salespeople with top quartile talent sold 12 percent more than those with bottom quartile talent. They were all doing the same job. They all got the same training. But they did not bring the same level of talent to the role. And the ones with more of the right talent took that same investment of training and turned it into measurably better performance.

That 12 percent difference in sales performance equated to $1.7 million in increased sales for this sample of the retailer's salespeople over a three-month period. What would happen if the retailer extended the impact of top talent to their entire salesforce? Based on the size of the study relative to the size of their overall salesforce and extending the findings from that one quarter to an entire fiscal year, the company could conservatively realize $15 million in additional sales revenue each year by matching the right training to the right people.

LESSON

Talent (aptitude) matters. Motivation and training alone are not enough. Unless someone has the talent for a particular role, all the training and practice in the world will not enable them to achieve excellence.

In the previous example, everyone got the same investment of training, but the people with the right talent made the most of it—in a way that drove measurable business growth. As a manager, how can you match the right people with the right training to achieve the right results? Assessment instruments can help, but so can a good eye and patient observation. This story provides a clear illustration and a concrete strategy:

The Diving Horses

In 1979, I went to Atlantic City to serve on the opening team of the Playboy Hotel and Casino. The city was a boomtown, bustling with activity. Numerous casinos were under construction. The energy and excitement were palpable. It was a heady time. Atlantic City was being reborn.

In conversation with a long-time resident, I learned that in days gone by, diving horses had been a major attraction along the once-famous boardwalk. A horse and rider would walk up a long ramp to a high platform that extended over the ocean, and they would jump off. Voluntarily! Diving horses.

Immediately, I became intensely curious about how one trains a horse to do that. My acquaintance said, "Well, the horse trainer still lives here, and he is often at the Good Times bar at 5:30 on weekdays. You could just go over there and ask him."

Unbelievable. Sometimes, life just hands you something good.

I was soon sitting there with the trainer. I wish I could remember his name. This is what he told me:

"I don't actually train them. I find them. I take very young horses to the beach. Some of them just like going into the water. They just go in spontaneously, and they like it. The horses that don't go in, I eliminate. I take the ones who liked the water to a very low pier. Some jump in. The others I eliminate. I take the ones who jumped in to a slightly higher pier. Every once in a while, I find a horse that likes jumping off the high platform. Of course at every stage there is some coaxing, there is some rewarding. But there is never any coercion. That's how it's done. That's my secret."

Years later, I was listening to a famous animal trainer who worked with lions and tigers. The interviewer asked how he trained those cats to perform the specific tricks. He replied, "I watch them when they're very young—watch them when they're just playing, doing whatever they want. Different cats like doing different things. If a particular cat likes to jump backward, I create a trick that requires him to jump backward. I build the tricks around what they naturally like to do."

Alexander Lacey, the big cat trainer and presenter for Ringling Brothers and Barnum & Bailey Circus summarizes the idea simply and powerfully: "You have to see what they like to do, what they are best at, and then you work on that."

The same principles apply to people.

LESSON

If you find out what a person does naturally and likes to do, providing training in those areas will likely result in rapid growth and increased engagement. If you are training someone to do something for which they have no affinity (e.g., diving off a high platform or selling luxury cosmetics)

(continued)

(*continued*)

you can make some progress, but it will not be rapid, it will not be easy, and it will plateau long before their performance could be called excellent. Their engagement will also likely go in the wrong direction.

There are plenty of situations in which a person has not yet tried something, so neither they nor anyone else knows whether they have an affinity for it. In that case, give it a try. But after a while, if progress is slow and labored, if they do not enjoy it, continuing is not good for them or for the organization. They know they are not succeeding. Leaving them there is not kind. Quit wasting time, effort, and money. Find something that is a better fit.

EXPERIMENT: MATCH THE RIGHT PEOPLE TO THE RIGHT TRAINING

1. Identify an employee who is genuinely trying but still not performing up to your expectations, despite their efforts and yours.
2. Ask yourself whether additional efforts will bear fruit.
3. If the answer is "No," do not allow them to struggle in that position.
4. Look for a way to train that person that is more consistent with what he or she does naturally and enjoys most.
5. If the preceding step fails, find something different for that person to learn—something that is a better fit.
6. Pay attention to the reaction of your other employees, and pay attention to what happens next for this person. You might well be pleasantly surprised.

DELEGATE TO THE RIGHT PEOPLE

Newly promoted supervisors and managers often struggle with delegation, and they are not the only ones. Almost without exception, people who become managers were once outstanding individual performers. They know they can perform certain tasks with excellence, but, to be optimally effective as managers, they must trust others to perform those same tasks. This shift in what it takes to succeed pushes many managers outside their comfort zones. Are you in this situation?

Learning more about how to delegate can certainly help, but it is much more important to learn as much as possible about your people. Just as betting on talent helps you find the right players for your team, identifying the right person will make you most successful at delegation. And the right person is not only someone who has the aptitude to do the task with excellence, but also someone you trust.

The first part, finding the right aptitude, may be the easiest part. Like the best coaches and trainers, you should build your plays around your players. First, think about who will do the task with excellence. The more you know about each of your people, the easier it will be to make this decision. Make sure you know:

1. Their strengths and weaknesses
2. What they are passionate about
3. What motivates them
4. What their career goals are
5. Whether they will find this assignment attractive and engaging

If you know these things about each of the people on your team, you will be able to match the right person to the right task or responsibility and create an optimal fit. When you make a good match, you will have confidence in that person's capability and motivation to perform with excellence. But going one step further will make you an even better delegator.

This additional step may be more difficult, as it is a question of trust. Assess your personal relationship with each individual on your team. How close are you to these people? Aside from the aptitude and fit considerations, how much do you trust each person? If trust is low, knowing all there is to know about a person's strengths, weaknesses, motivations, and goals is not enough to ensure successful delegation. Why? Because if trust is low, you will not be able to fully release responsibility to that person. You will constantly wonder whether, despite the person's capability and motivation, she will follow through and be loyal to you, or put the interests of the team above her own interests. If trust is low, ask yourself, "Why do I not trust this person?" and, "Am I willing to work on building trust?" If you cannot both identify why trust is low and also do whatever it takes to increase trust with a member of your team, you will never effectively delegate responsibility to that person.

Delegation always involves risk. No amount of knowledge about how to delegate will eliminate this risk. People will make mistakes. Things will go wrong. But when trust is high, you will know that mistakes are innocent, not calculated. In the context of that trust, when you delegate to the right people, based on what they do best, you will find that they do some things even better than you would have done. When it comes to delegation, that is where the treasure is buried.

LESSON

Delegation always involves risk. The key is selecting the right person. Delegate to a person who has the right strengths and motivation to perform the assignment with excellence, and trust that person to deliver.

Growth always involves going outside your comfort zone. You might be apprehensive about delegating, but you do not have to let that feeling control your behavior. Identify the right person, build trust, and take a risk. Where would you be today if someone had not taken a risk on you?

EXPERIMENT: TAKE A RISK

1. Identify at least two things you are doing yourself that really should be delegated.
2. Identify two people on your team whom you trust and who have the right strengths to do those things with excellence.

3. Take a chance. Delegate to those people.
4. Understand that they will not do it the way you did it. Understand that they will make some mistakes.
5. Resist the urge to take those things back.
6. Watch for them to do some things even better than you might have done them.
7. After 90 days, reflect on how taking a risk has worked out for you and for the people on your team.

ASK FOR COMMITMENT

R emember the old joke about the tourist asking the New Yorker how to get to Carnegie Hall? The well-known reply is, "Practice, practice, practice." Practice requires sacrifice. As John C. Maxwell reminds us, talent is never enough. In an interview with a self-made billionaire, the interviewer asked, "What is the secret to success?" The billionaire replied, "It's quite simple. Decide what you want to achieve and what you're willing to give up to get it."

To achieve greatness, people must be willing to make sacrifices. Michael Phelps and Michael Jordan, for example, were known for their remarkable work ethics. Achieving greatness as a team also requires sacrifice, and extraordinary teams can only emerge when individuals are willing to commit to an extraordinary level of sacrifice.

LESSON

Achieving extraordinary outcomes requires team members who willingly make sacrifices involving long hours, extra effort, and the burden of additional stress. This requires an exceptional kind of person.

This level of commitment goes way beyond mere engagement. You cannot install it. You must select for it. Look for people with the right aptitude for high commitment. Make a high level of commitment a critical element of fit when you select people to join your team and when you delegate tasks and responsibilities.

EXPERIMENT: INTERVIEW FOR WILLINGNESS TO SACRIFICE

1. Be clear that this opportunity is not for everyone.
2. Be blunt about the challenges and the sacrifices that will be required to meet those challenges. Give examples. Tell stories to illustrate what you mean.
3. Ask candidates to tell you about sacrifices they've made in the past, and why they did so. Ask why they might make similar (or even greater) sacrifices if they joined your team. Is there something about the mission or the rewards that would evoke the desire to sacrifice?
4. Allow people to self-select out. Someone who is just looking for a job will not make the sacrifices required.
5. When you have hired a couple of people who gave you good answers to these questions, reflect on whether their commitment lives up to what they said.

INVEST YOUR TIME WITH TOP PERFORMERS

Dr. William E. Hall articulated a concept he called the "Law of Parsimony." We have only 24 hours in a day, so we cannot invest in everyone. We must choose thoughtfully with whom we spend our time. As a manager, what choices are you making now?

We often hear the maxim, "A team is only as strong as its weakest player." This myth is repeated so frequently that many managers accept it as true. Consequently, poor performers often receive the lion's share of time and attention. Some modest improvements are gained, but what would happen if that same amount of time and attention were focused on the best performers? Simply put, you will get a much higher return on time, effort, and money.

Once again, we encounter the difference between room for improvement and potential for improvement. Counterintuitively, your top performers have the most potential for improvement. Therefore, if you want to bring about the greatest gains in your team's performance, invest the majority of your time with your top performers (and with high-potential rookies).

And by the way, who do you think your competitors want to recruit—your best people or your worst people? If you pay more attention to poor performers than to top performers, you are making those top performers more receptive to new opportunities. Does this strike you as wise? In addition to yielding the greatest performance improvements, investing more of your time with top performers also makes them less vulnerable to being recruited away.

Take the time to develop close relationships with your top performers. This conveys significance and enables you to discover what kinds of investment will be most meaningful to those people. When you spend more time with your top performers, you will increase their loyalty and enhance the likelihood of retaining them.

This does not mean you should ignore your poor performers. It does mean that if you are going to spend more time with some people than with others, the people who get more of your time should be your top performers, not your bottom ones.

LESSON

Invest the lion's share of your time with your top performers. You will see the greatest improvements in team performance, and you will make those valuable employees less vulnerable to being recruited away.

EXPERIMENT: HUMAN INVESTMENT PLANNING

1. Fold an 8½-by-11-inch piece of paper in half, lengthwise, creating two columns.
2. In the left-hand column, force-rank the employees on your team, putting the name of the best employee at the top of the page, the second best next, and so on, with your worst employee last. This might involve some tough decisions, but don't agonize over it. It does not have to be perfect. Don't spend more than five minutes making this list.
3. In the right-hand column, rank those same employees, putting the name of the person with whom you spend the most time at the top, the one who is second in terms of your time next, and so on to the employee with whom you spend the least amount of time. You will have the same names in each column, but they might be in a different order.
4. Draw lines from each name in the left-hand column to that same name in the right-hand column. For example, if Joe Smith is one of your employees, his name will appear in both columns. Draw a line from Joe Smith in the left-hand column to Joe Smith in the right-hand column. Do this for each name on the list.
5. Examine the connecting lines. Are they straight across and parallel for the most part? Or do they look like a bunch of Xs?
6. If they are straight across and parallel, you are spending most of your time with the right people. If they look like a bunch of Xs, make a conscious effort to spend more time with your top performers and less time with your poor performers.

CONDUCT OCCASIONAL TEAM-BUILDING EVENTS

Offsite team-building events are expensive, often involving costs for travel, meals, lodging, and professional facilitators. The biggest cost is the salaries of the participants. As a manager, you must ensure that these events create enough value to justify the investment of time, effort, and money.

First, be clear about the goals and outcomes you want from an offsite team-building event. It is not unusual for a leader to say something like, "Larry, I need some team building. Can you facilitate a half-day for me?"

"Team building" means different things to different people. So I ask some questions.

1. Why do you need a team-building event?
2. What do you hope to accomplish?
3. When it is over, if we are wildly successful, what will be different in the workplace?

LESSON

When planning an offsite team-building event, clarify the outcomes you want to achieve.

Once you have clarified what you want to accomplish and why, you can move on to the most important step in this process: selecting the right facilitator. Your success will depend less on the agenda and more on the facilitator. Whether or not you accomplish your goals depends entirely on the talent of the facilitator. Because each team is unique, each of these events takes on a life of its own. A talented facilitator is attuned to the group and can sense when to detour from the planned agenda. A great facilitator can recognize an important moment, and knows how to capitalize on it. The most valuable team-building events often take major detours from the planned agenda.

Be realistic about what can be accomplished in this type of event. You are not going to magically change your team culture. At best, you might achieve a breakthrough upon which you can build. Near the conclusion of the event, call for commitments about what each person will do differently when they return to the workplace.

LESSON

The most important decision about an offsite team-building event is who will facilitate it. The talent of the facilitator is the most important factor in the success of the meeting.

Keep in mind that you can achieve meaningful team building without a facilitator or an expensive retreat. There are plenty of low-cost team-building possibilities available to every group. Find some community volunteer activities your team can do together. Celebrate important life events together. Create a team book club. Create a team discussion night in which you informally brainstorm and discuss ideas and possible strategies for improvement—no flip charts, no minutes, no follow up—just discussion of ideas. Do a joke night after work. Cook together—there is something ancient and powerful about cooking and sharing a meal. The possibilities are endless.

LESSON

Great team-building events do not require an outside facilitator or an expensive offsite retreat. With a modicum of creativity, you can create a variety of team-building events that will not break the bank.

EXPERIMENT: CONDUCT AN INEXPENSIVE TEAM-BUILDING EVENT

1. Write down the outcomes you would like to achieve. It can be a simple as, "Have fun together and enhance relationships."
2. Think up the team-building activity you think will accomplish those outcomes. Some ideas are listed in this chapter, and you can generate more. Pick one.
3. Pick someone on your team to organize and conduct the activity. It can be you, but it can also be another team member. Think about talent. Is there someone on your team who is really good at planning events or has special interests and expertise in the kind of activity you will be doing?
4. Conduct the activity.
5. Assess the results. Did you accomplish your goals? What went well? What will you do differently next time?

Remember, team-building events can add a lot of value, but team building should occur every day. This is your responsibility. Ensure the team is aligned around clear goals and values. Hold people accountable to enliven those values and to fulfill their responsibilities. Make sure each person understands and appreciates the strengths of his or her teammates. Encourage people to ask each other for help. Set the standard for caring deeply and authentically for each person on your team.

When a team is aligned around its goals and values, when people appreciate one another's strengths, and when people care deeply and authentically about one another, amazing things can happen.

ADVANCE FROM TEAM TO FAMILY

Team-building events provide opportunities for teams to experience, briefly, the tangible esprit de corps that is the norm among extraordinary teams. If you have been a member of an extraordinary team, you know what it feels like. And you know that it goes beyond a single event to define how everyday interactions feel among the members of the team.

This book began with a focus on the importance of relationships. Remember the story from Chapter 1 about Bernie and the diner? Team members who enjoy close relationships truly care about one another. They go the extra mile to support one another, and this caring and commitment contributes to an extraordinary team.

Members of extraordinary teams become friends—or more. As the quality of their relationships grows, they start to think and talk about the team as family. Referring to their team as family is not just a slogan, either. They mean it.

As a manager, if you want to build an extraordinary team, help your people create strong bonds. Help them get to know one another. Create opportunities for them to explore these kinds of questions:

1. What is going on in their lives outside the team?
2. What are their dreams, aspirations, and life challenges?
3. What are their interests?
4. What are their needs?
5. What are their unique gifts?

Create opportunities to socialize outside of work and invite significant others to be part of those occasions. The importance of including significant others cannot be overstated. That is what families do, right? Celebrate important events together, like graduations, personal achievements, engagements, and the birth of a child. Support one another during illness, death, and other challenging life events. Be present for the highs and the lows. Care about each other. Make frequent use of the following phrase, "How can I help?"

Quit asking people to change. Make accepting people as they are an explicit value your team shares. We all have aces and spaces. Encourage your team members to accept one another with all their strengths and all their flaws. True friends allow people to be themselves. Focus on what is right about people. Focus on how they can make their best contribution to the team. Foster a culture in which people build others up instead of looking for ways to tear others down.

If you help people build close, positive relationships, if you help them cultivate genuine friendships, the teamwork will improve. As you strive together to attain your goals, you will go through ups and downs together, and these shared experiences will deepen the relationships. If you can do this, the intangible rewards of the journey might create value for the members of your team that even exceeds the tangible rewards of accomplishing the goal.

EXPERIMENT: CREATE SOCIAL EVENTS

1. If you are not good at thinking up fun, engaging social events for your team members, delegate this to someone who enjoys doing it.
2. Implement at least one social event per month in which each employee can bring a guest.
3. Do this for six months.
4. After six months, reflect on what you have learned. How has this affected the relationships and the teamwork?

AVOID THE PETER PRINCIPLE

In 1969, Laurence Peter and Raymond Hull wrote a wonderful book titled, *The Peter Principle: Why Things Always Go Wrong*. They pointed out that high individual performance is not evidence of potential to be a great supervisor. They observed that companies that base promotions on performance in the current job create a system in which all managers eventually rise to their level of incompetence.

The solution to this dilemma begins with the insight that there is a difference between performance in the current role and potential for high performance in the next step up the ladder because different roles require different talents and skills. To give a specific example, the role of sales manager requires different talents and skills from the role of sales representative. But, as Peter observed, the number one sales rep most often gets promoted to sales manager. Often—sadly, very often in the world of sales—the newly promoted individual is not a good manager. The company suffers a double whammy. They have taken their best sales rep off the playing field *and* they have given the team a poor manager. This is not a formula to build an extraordinary team.

LESSON

Different jobs require different talents. High individual performance is not evidence of potential to perform with excellence as a supervisor.

Just as putting someone in a bad fit has undesirable consequences, efforts to avoid the Peter Principle can also bring unpleasant consequences. When it comes to the Peter Principle, sometimes you are damned if you do and damned if you don't. Here is an example:

> ### Not Promoting Neil
>
> In the late 1980s, I was vice president of human resources for the Portman Hotel Company, and we were opening a hotel in San Francisco. When the hotel director of sales and marketing resigned, Neil, the number one sales rep, walked into the general manager's office and asked to be promoted to director, which was a long-standing career goal of his. Such a promotion also represented a typical career progression for that industry.
>
> Several executives, including the company president, interviewed Neil for the job. We all came to the conclusion that he was not a good fit for a management role. I was elected to deliver the bad news. I told Neil that we loved him in a sales role, but we did not see him as a good fit for a management role. He was very disappointed.
>
> Within 30 days Neil found a job as director of sales and marketing for a competitor. We lost our number one sales rep. I knew there was a good chance we would lose him if we did not give him the promotion. If we had promoted him, he would not have been a sales rep any more, and he would not have been a good manager, either. Losing him was much better than "Peter Principling" him.
>
> To this day, I sleep well with that decision. We did the right thing for the business. Neil would not have been a great manager. He would not have created extraordinary teams through his management and the business would not have reaped the benefits a better manager could deliver. Not only was it the best decision for the business, but also we did not put Neil into a bad fit, which might have caused stress-related illness or other ill effects for him personally.

Once you recognize the difference between performance and potential and start looking through the lens of potential, something really interesting can happen. You will notice that some employees who are not stars in their current roles have the potential to be excellent supervisors. They are better coaches than players. And when they have an opportunity to take the next step into a management role, they will become top-performing managers because that role fits so well with their potential.

LESSON

In considering people for promotion, shift from focusing on performance to focusing on potential. Make sure candidates have the potential to excel in the new role. When people are in the right fit, they spend most of their time doing things they are good at and enjoy. These candidates are energized by their job, not oppressed by it. Everybody wins.

EXPERIMENT: LOOK BEYOND CURRENT PERFORMANCE

1. Identify employees who:
   a. Enjoy teaching other employees.
   b. Always seem to care about the well-being of other employees.
   c. Make the workplace more fun.
   d. Always contribute to a positive atmosphere.
   e. Make suggestions for improvement.
   f. Are natural leaders.
2. When an opening occurs, put one of those employees into a supervisory role, even if he or she is not the best individual performer.
3. After 90 days, assess how this has worked. How has it affected your team and your team's results?

This discussion brings to light a more fundamental issue in our society. There is a widely held point of view that if one is not getting promoted, something is wrong. We need to eradicate this perception. This causes people to seek promotions for the wrong reasons, and attain roles that are not a good fit. They are driven to embody the Peter Principle. We need to ensure that people do not need a promotion to feel truly valued and significant.

DON'T LEAD PEOPLE ON

During the course of your career as a manager, you will inevitably have to speak with someone who aspires to a certain role in your organization, even though he or she does not have the natural talent to perform that role with excellence. You are committed to avoiding the Peter Principle. You will not promote people to the level of their incompetence. You should not lead people on. You must have difficult conversations in these instances. But what do you say? How do you help people work through the difference between their goals and reality as you see it? Every situation is unique, so we cannot give you a script. But we can provide an example and give you some guidelines.

Larry's Conversation with Joe

I was consulting for Lewis, a highly successful real estate developer, who was building a five-star resort in Arizona. His general counsel, Joe, was a real estate attorney whose career aspiration was to become a real estate developer himself, a dealmaker rather than "just" the attorney on these deals. Lewis had made a commitment that Joe would become a developer after the completion of this project.

By the time I came into the picture, Lewis had changed his mind about Joe. He did not believe Joe would do a good job as a developer. Lewis was quite pleased with Joe's performance as an attorney, but he thought Joe had an aversion to confrontation that would prevent him from closing real estate deals. He asked me for a second opinion.

(*continued*)

(continued)

I spent a lot of time getting to know Joe, to understand his themes and talents. I agreed with Lewis's assessment. It would not be good for Joe or for the company to let him become a developer.

Lewis really cared for Joe and felt terrible about not following through on his commitment. I asked Lewis if I could speak to Joe about it, and he agreed.

I met Joe in his office, which was in a construction trailer. I started the conversation by telling him that I recommended against the career move from attorney to developer. I pointed out that he was so averse to confrontation that when he was in private practice, he had a hard time asking clients to pay their bills. Sometimes he did not ask at all and did not get paid. I helped him think about the daily confrontations that real estate developers experience. They have to deal with neighbors, city councils, construction workers, employees, suppliers, and more. Every day. I said I did not think he would like that necessary part of the job and that he would find it to be very stressful. It would not be a good fit.

I concluded by telling Joe how much Lewis appreciated his work as an attorney. Lewis was impressed in particular with Joe's creativity in finding ways to overcome legal hurdles to getting deals done. Furthermore, Lewis admired the way Joe could keep track of the many details and documents (we're talking thousands of pages) involved in complex real estate transactions. Lewis valued Joe and was willing to invest resources to help Joe grow in his current role.

Joe listened attentively, but it was tough to hear. He was angry. He threw me out of his office.

A couple of days later, I returned to meet with Lewis, and when I arrived, Lewis's assistant told me that Joe wanted to see me. She asked me to meet with Joe first and then come back to Lewis.

I walked over to Joe's office, expecting the worst. But I got a pleasant surprise. Joe told me that after a couple of long conversations with his wife, he had come to the conclusion that we were right. To become a developer would be a bad fit for him. He did not want a role that involved daily, often unpleasant, confrontations. He was proud of the talents that Lewis and I had recognized in him. And he released Lewis from his commitment.

If someone on your team does not have a natural talent for the role he aspires to, it is not in anyone's interest to cast that person in that role. The ideal outcome would be that the employee is not given the aspirational role, understands why (even if disagreeing with the reasoning), and remains an engaged contributor in a role in which he can be successful—one with a career arc more suited to his natural talents.

If you are the manager delivering the bad news, remember that people almost always accept the final decision—it is the process they complain about. There is no way they are going to feel good about what you have to say in the moment. Sugarcoating it will not help. Be transparent, clear, and compassionate. Listen actively. If you sincerely have employees' best interests at heart, they will know that. And they will know it if you do not have their best interests at heart, too.

Start by asking why he seeks this role. Listen, listen, and listen some more. Give some feedback showing that you understand his thoughts and feelings.

Then discuss what his life would be like on a day-to-day basis. Help him visualize it. Remember, you are delivering the bad news that he does not have strong talent for the role he seeks. The role will likely require him to engage frequently in activities that he does not enjoy. For example, suppose he aspires to become a manager. Does he want to sit in meetings half the day? Does he want to be accountable for the performance of others? Does he want to spend a lot of time on administrative paperwork? Does he want to work the hours required in this role? Does he want to confront unacceptable work performance? Forcing him into activities that are not aligned with what he enjoys will be stressful.

LESSON

When people are in the wrong fit for their talent, they will experience a lot of stress, which will cause physical and emotional problems. It is not just bad for the organization, it is bad for the individuals.

As this person's manager, do the caring thing and say, "I don't think that role is the best fit for you. I don't think you'll like doing those activities, and I don't think it'll be good for you."

If there is a role in which this person can excel, discuss the importance of that role in the company. Help the person understand why that other role is better suited to his or her talents. Paint a picture of how investing in his or her strengths can make a bigger difference or lead to greater growth.

If it is clear to you that the person will never get that aspirational role, be willing to say, "Honestly, I don't think that's in your future here. I think we have associates whose talent is more suitable for that role, so I think you'll be out-competed when opportunities open up. I know this is hard to hear, but I want to be honest with you." Do not lead him or her on.

In these types of situations, you are going to win some and lose some. Good employees will leave your team for companies that are willing to give them that aspirational role. Have no regrets because the alternative—giving him or her the role—is worse for the employee, worse for your team, worse for your company, and worse for your customers.

EXPERIMENT: DEALING WITH SOMEONE WHOSE ASPIRATIONS DO NOT MATCH HIS OR HER TALENT

1. Remember that this is a tough message to hear.
2. Avoid sugarcoating your answer. Be as kind as possible, but be clear and straightforward.
3. Listen. Listen. Listen.
4. Accept the consequences. Do not give someone a role that is a bad fit just to keep that person from leaving.

Chapter 41

SOMETIMES FIRING SOMEONE IS THE CARING THING TO DO

If you are committed to building an extraordinary team, the people on your team are likely to be full of determination and willing to push themselves hard to succeed. The kind of people you want for your team are the kind of people who never quit. But what happens when their determination and grit drives them to continue striving for a goal they will never achieve because it does not fit with their talent, even when doing so makes them miserable and negatively affects their happiness or even their health? An example from sports may help:

Professional Boxers Don't Quit

Boxing is a dangerous sport. The primary job of the referee is to ensure the safety of two combatants who are aggressively trying to hurt each other to the point that one of them will be unable to continue. The winner is the last person standing. Stepping into the ring takes a considerable amount of courage. It is also a "sudden death" kind of sport. Even if a boxer seems to be losing decisively, one good punch can turn the tide and win the fight.

I recently watched a fight in which the two boxers were not equally matched. One guy was getting the living daylights beat out of him. But he was a professional boxer—full of courage, determination, and heart. He

(continued)

(*continued*)

would not give up. Eventually, even though both men were still standing, the trainer of the overmatched boxer threw in the towel, ending the fight. Sometimes, *you cannot leave the decision to quit up to the boxer himself.* When a boxer will not quit but will be seriously (even perhaps fatally) injured by continuing, the trainer and the referee are responsible for making the decision for him. This was one of those times.

Is someone who reports to you in this situation? If you care about that person, do the right thing. It is what trainers do when they care deeply about their fighters. It is what you should do if you truly care about your employee. Sometimes, like a trainer, you have to throw in the towel. Sometimes you have to recognize when you have reached a point where it goes against the best interests of the employee or the business to fight on.

LESSON

To build an extraordinary team, sometimes you have to let someone go.

How do you know when the time has come to throw in the towel and let someone go? Ask yourself these questions:

1. Have you taught, coached, and given the employee ample time to learn?
2. Has the employee tried his or her best?
3. Does the situation require behaviors that are not in the employee's repertoire? Do you believe, in your heart of hearts, that additional effort will turn the situation around?

It is not time until you know—in your heart of hearts—that you have done everything you can to help that person succeed. Before you get to that point, you must communicate bluntly and clearly that her employment cannot continue unless performance improves. You must listen to her side of the story. You must communicate just as clearly and passionately that you are an ally and will do everything in your power to help her succeed. It is not time until you have delivered on that promise, until you have put in extra effort and really extended yourself. When all of that has gone before, on the day you realize that additional efforts will not lead to success, then you know it is time. And you must act accordingly.

LESSON

In the vast majority of cases, *when an employee is not succeeding, he or she knows it long before you do.* If you can't help that person succeed, leaving him or her in that situation is *not* a kind or compassionate thing to do. Doing so will start to diminish the employee's self-esteem. If it goes on for too long, the stress could cause health problems. Do not be a party to that. As unpleasant and painful as it might be, have the conversation. Despite the pain, it is the most caring and compassionate thing you can do in this situation.

How do you fire someone professionally and compassionately? Begin with the stance that when you have to fire someone, it is as much your own failure as it is your employee's. It was either a mistake in the hiring decision (you selected someone without the right aptitude or did not ensure the right fit), or you did not ensure that the person was trained and supervised in a way that helped him or her succeed. This is a shared failure. But as the manager, you must do your job and take responsibility for letting the person go.

LESSON

Other employees are watching. They correctly assume this is how you will treat them if they ever find themselves in the same situation. Furthermore, if one employee is not succeeding, other employees know it too. It is affecting them, and they expect you to do your job and take care of it.

When you initiate the conversation, do not start with small talk about the weather or a recent sporting event. Get into the meat of the issue right away. Briefly review the expectations and the shortfall in performance. Tell the person it is not working out (which she probably already knows) and that it is time for her to leave. If you are sorry, say so, but in this situation, apologize only if you really mean it.

This might be painful for you, and it might present you with some challenges in your organization, but for the person being fired, it is a life-changing event. Compassion is mandatory. Explain the separation process. Answer any questions. But do not extend the moment. After your conversation, proceed to the next step.

CRITICAL LESSON

This does not have to be end of your relationship with this person. You can continue to care about him or her.

Your next step can be helping in the search for the employee's next job. The best outcome is that she finds something soon and goes on to have great success. Many managers are fortunate to maintain positive relationships with people they have fired and can continue to support their success as they move forward in their careers. But a manager must take that first and hardest step. When it is time for an employee to leave, do not delay in taking action, as unpleasant as it might be. Do it with compassion, and own your failure to help that person succeed. And remember, you can continue to care about and support her even though she no longer works for you.

EXPERIMENT: TAKE ACTION WHEN SOMEONE IS NOT SUCCEEDING

1. Identify an employee who is not succeeding.
2. State your performance expectations clearly, including a time frame.
3. State the consequences of not performing up to expectations.
4. Listen to his or her side of the story.
5. State that you are committed to help that employee succeed.
6. Fulfill your commitments 100 percent.
7. If and when you reach a point at which additional efforts will not lead to success, take action. Begin the process of terminating that person's employment with you.

NEVER BADMOUTH TOP PERFORMERS WHO RESIGN

E ven extraordinary teams are not perfectly stable. Occasionally you have to let someone go. On the flip side, occasionally one of your top people resigns. It is understandable that a manager feels unhappy when a top performer resigns. The employee is intentionally ending the relationship, so there is an element of personal rejection involved, especially in cases in which the manager has invested heavily in that person's development. Also, the manager needs to replace that person now, which could be a daunting challenge given that the person is so good. As a result, the top performer who resigns is often treated poorly. Sometimes, after the employee has left, the manager may speak negatively about that person. What are the consequences of these types of behavior?

Remember, other employees pay close attention in these situations. Before the resignation, it is likely that the manager spoke highly of this person. If that same manager now speaks poorly about that person after he or she leaves, the manager's reputation is diminished. Employees can readily see that such behavior is both unprofessional and unnecessary. Respect for the manager is diminished. Trust is also diminished.

When trust is diminished, employees may begin to worry that if they give a standard notice of resignation, the manager may terminate them immediately, causing economic hardship. So when they are exploring career possibilities outside the company, they keep it secret. The resignation comes as an unpleasant surprise. This leads to a harsh response from the manager, which reinforces this destructive cycle of cause and effect.

As a manager, how can you break this cycle?

First, let go of the attitude that exploring career possibilities outside the company is an act of disloyalty. Let your people know that when career opportunities come to their attention, it is okay with you for them to explore those opportunities. They do not have to hide it. If you really care about your people, you will want the best for them (and for their families). There will be times when another company presents such a great opportunity that you can't compete with it. Encourage people to speak with you about these opportunities. This gives you the chance to make changes that may move them to stay.

Second, consider the resignation a sort of graduation. It is likely that the investments you have made in this top performer have prepared him for this new position. He should leave with your blessing and sincere wishes for success in the new job. This type of response demonstrates that you genuinely want the best for that person, and it maintains your positive, supportive relationship. It might be that a year or two from now, you will have a terrific opportunity for this person to come back. If your relationship is good, you will be in a position to recruit him back.

What benefits will you enjoy if you break the negative cycle?

1. Top performers will let you know when they are looking, giving you an opportunity to better meet their needs, and you will be able to start thinking about how to replace them, if necessary.
2. You will avoid diminishing the trust and respect people have for you.
3. This person will speak positively about you in the community.
4. You will be in a position to recruit this person back.
5. Word will get around in your community that you invest in people so they can advance in their careers and that you sincerely care about them as people. *More people and better people will want to work for you.* That could be the pot of gold at the end of this rainbow.

LESSON

You can break the cycle of negativity that often occurs when a valued employee leaves.

EXPERIMENT: STOP TALKING NEGATIVELY ABOUT EMPLOYEES WHO LEAVE

1. The next time someone leaves you, say only positive things about that person.
2. Do not tolerate others saying negative things.
3. Treat the experience like a graduation.
4. Maintain a good relationship with the one who is leaving.
5. Pay attention to how people respond.

Chapter 43

DON'T ALWAYS TAKE THE EASY WAY OUT

I n the previous two chapters, we addressed the reality that, even among high-performing teams, turnover is sometimes unavoidable. Top performers resign. Despite everyone's best efforts, some people will never perform at an acceptable level, and it becomes necessary to let them go. Life is messy. Sometimes, circumstances justify letting someone go, and firing someone might be the most obvious response, but it is not always the best course of action. How do you manage to make a difference in those kinds of situations? Here is a story to illustrate:

The Stolen Mink Coats

It was Christmas season. Our hotel was decorated within an inch of its life. We had roaring fireplaces filling the atmosphere with warmth and that wonderful aroma you can get only from burning real wood. We had live Christmas music. Every function room was hosting a holiday party. Guests were dressed to the nines—tuxedos, evening gowns, minks, and shminks. For a hotelier, evenings like this are quite memorable. This evening became memorable for all the wrong reasons.

One party experienced a serious misfortune. Five mink coats were stolen from our coat check closet. Two of these coats were irreplaceable family heirlooms. Our investigation revealed that James, one of our banquet captains, pulled the coat check person from her post to help pour coffee for about 15 minutes. During that brief window of time, the coats were

(continued)

(continued)

stolen. The thieves probably strolled right out the front door with them. On this evening, no observer would have given it a second thought.

James's poor judgment cost our hotel thousands of dollars and damaged our reputation. As the general manager, I could have fired him, and I was getting pressure from the corporate office to do just that. The HR people were concerned about consistency and precedent. Branding and PR people felt that firing him rapidly would send a positive message about the hotel's reputation. Others wanted him fired just because they were angry.

I decided not to fire James. He was one of the most talented banquet captains with whom I ever had the pleasure to work. Leadership, people skills, professional knowledge, bearing—he had it all. He had worked for our hotel for many years. Over those years, numerous guests told us they booked business with us specifically because they knew James would take care of them with excellence. His error in this case was egregious, but James had never done anything like this before.

I had a rather stern discussion with him. He felt terrible and fully expected to be fired. I put a written warning in his file, and explained why I was not inclined to fire him when I balanced his overall value to the hotel against this one instance of poor judgment. Tears surfaced. By the end of the conversation, I had rehired him emotionally (see more on emotional rehiring in Chapter 52).

Decisions have consequences. Not firing James did in fact create some risks associated with consistency of discipline. Also, many people felt that he needed to be held accountable. They disagreed quite vigorously with the decision to retain him, and many readers may disagree as well. On the other hand, the hotel retained a very valuable employee. James became even more loyal to the hotel and to me as his manager. All the hotel's employees got a clear demonstration of how they would be treated in a similar situation. They also got a message about loyalty. They knew that, as their manager, I had their backs.

I have several of these stories. One of them is about when my former boss, Phil Lombardi, refused to accept my resignation for a major mistake that wasted a lot of money, and caused him serious loss of face. That may be why I take this point of view. I learned and grew from that experience.

Sometimes, firing someone for egregiously poor judgment is the right thing to do. But too often a manager fires someone because it is the easy way out. The extreme version of this is called "scapegoating."

Do any of us think we go through life without occasionally exercising poor judgment, and sometimes very poor judgment? Some of these occasions present opportunities for learning and growth. As a manager, be on the lookout for those kinds of opportunities.

LESSON

The fact that you would be justified in firing someone does not mean that doing so is the best course of action.

SHAPE YOUR CULTURE

FOCUS ON THE RIGHT THINGS

M anaging to make a difference involves creating a culture that encourages people to become their best selves. Culture can be a slippery concept. Read any description of "great organizations" and you will find a laundry list of customs, beliefs, rituals, and perks touted as elements of their unique cultures—unlimited vacation, Ping Pong tables and pinball machines in brainstorming rooms, food trucks on Fridays, nap rooms to recharge. The list goes on. It can suck you in to focusing on the wrong things if you let it.

BEWARE!

Customs, beliefs, rituals, and perks become signs and expressions of cultural values. Understanding them helps to describe the culture. But they do not create and shape culture. Picking up practices from one team or organization and plunking them down into yours is not a great strategy for shaping your culture. Too often, looking from the outside in, even the best managers and leaders can miss that point.

For example, the "quality circle" became a formalized part of the culture of many Japanese companies in the 1960s, and played a key role in enabling those companies to produce very high quality products, including automobiles and consumer electronics. Because of this success, many U.S.-based companies tried to plunk quality circles into their culture, but the strategy did not work. Quality circles did not harmonize with the typical U.S.-based company culture. The cultural context to embrace that approach did not exist.

We want to help you focus on the right things. Based on what you have read so far in this book, it should come as no surprise that we define "the right things" as people.

LESSON

Culture is shaped by the people an organization selects, develops, and retains.

If you want to shape your culture in ways that optimize performance and retention, you must start by focusing on the right things—your people—because culture arises organically from your people and your shared values. Culture is more than what you do or what you say. Culture is who you are. Questions like this can help you define key elements of your organization's culture:

1. What unifies both the veterans and the newest recruits?
2. What values drive them?
3. What makes people stay?
4. What attracts new people?
5. What are the common characteristics among our top performers?

By all means, look outside your organization for ideas and inspiration for how to mold and optimize culture. Every chapter in this section provides people-focused ideas and experiments you can try. But recognize that, ultimately, what you choose to incorporate has to fit your people, your shared values, and your history as an organization. Your organization has a culture now. Use the chapters in this section to amplify the best elements of your existing culture and to shape your culture in ways that optimize people's opportunities to become their best selves.

EXEMPLIFY CULTURAL VALUES IN EMPLOYEE ORIENTATION

M any organizations make employee orientation a mind-numbing review of the employee handbook. The best managers and organizations avoid that. They focus most of their time instead on helping new employees understand the values and beliefs of the organization, along with the expected behaviors. This approach is engaging. It allows people to decide whether their personal values harmonize with the organization's. It invites them to join emotionally, to get excited about what the organization stands for in the world, and ultimately to make a commitment to enliven those values through their work.

If you have a strong, clearly defined culture, it will not be for everyone. Ritz-Carlton and Zappos, for example, encourage people to opt out immediately if they are not excited about becoming a member. Zappos even offers new employees $2,000 if they wish to opt out.

For this to work, by the way, the description of cultural values cannot be fiction. When employees leave orientation, they experience the culture directly. If the difference between the described culture and the experienced culture is too great, disengagement sets in immediately.

When was the last time you reviewed your orientation and your handbook? Are you proud of the way they express your brand and exemplify your culture?

LESSON

Make sure your new employee orientation is not a mind-numbing experience. Make it a fun and engaging way for people to experience your culture.

EXPERIMENT: REDESIGN EMPLOYEE ORIENTATION

1. What could you do differently to make orientation a more fun and engaging experience? Seek outside ideas, if necessary. Make benchmark visits to other organizations to get ideas. But remember to make sure they harmonize with what is true about your culture, your people, your values, and your customs, beliefs, rituals, and perks.
2. Redesign orientation along those lines.
3. Reflect on what you have learned. How are your newest employees different after orientation now? Do they feel differently about joining your organization? Do they seem more ready to hit the ground running?

Chapter 46

WELCOME AND INTEGRATE NEW TEAM MEMBERS

For new team members, the first few days and weeks on the job set the stage for their entire tenure with you. Employee orientation helps acclimate people who are new to your organization, but you may also have an opportunity to welcome new people to your team who have already been with the organization for a while. Think about what happens when a new person joins your team.

- What is the experience like for that person?
- What is it like for current team members?
- What do you do to get that person comfortable and productive?
- What do you do to jumpstart trust and collaboration?

A seminar participant recounted her recent experience joining a new department in her organization. The other employees in the department were surprised to see her. They had no idea she was joining. Unfortunately, this experience is all too common. It affects your current team members negatively, too. As a manager, how can you make sure this never happens to anyone who is new to your team?

Many organizations have a formal orientation process for onboarding new hires, and research shows that effectively implementing those kinds of programs results in:

- Increased job satisfaction and commitment
- Improved retention

- Higher performance
- Lower stress[1]

You do not need a cumbersome, formal process, but you should be thoughtful and intentional in crafting the experience. We discussed a simple process in Chapter 13, and a simple, consistently applied process is likely to achieve outcomes similar to the ones found in the research. Cultivating relationships should be your number one priority in creating a fruitful onboarding experience. The more rapidly you can get positive relationships going, the more rapidly a person will become comfortable and productive. To get relationships going, people must get to know one another.

Make sure new people get invited to join team members at lunch, on breaks, and at social events outside of work. If there are no social gatherings planned, plan one. It can be as simple as an informal drink or a pizza after work. Make it part of your department's culture for current team members to go out of their way to make new team members feel welcome. In some cases, it might be helpful to appoint a "buddy" (not a supervisor) who can answer questions for a new person. Perhaps team members can connect with new people on social media like LinkedIn, Twitter, or Facebook.

If you do only what is in the preceding paragraph, you will create a more positive experience for the entire department, integrate new team members more rapidly, and enhance morale and productivity for your entire team. To create an even better welcome experience, conduct Focus On You (see Chapter 2) with new people and their team members during their first day or week.

Here is another effective technique from our own experience. Some years ago, we had a couple of team members who really enjoyed creating good-natured initiation experiences for new team members. For example, in one case, we filled someone's office, floor to ceiling, with balloons. In another, we wrapped everything in aluminum foil. The timing was crucial. We were wise enough not to do this right away. We waited a couple of weeks, after relationships had a chance to form. The message from these pranks was crystal clear: You are one of us now. Every new person just loved it!

LESSON

Whatever techniques work in your situation, be thoughtful and intentional about welcoming new team members. Cultivating relationships should be your number one priority. A fun welcoming process also serves as a team-building activity.

EXPERIMENT: WELCOME NEW TEAM MEMBERS

1. Work with your team to come up with fun, engaging ways to welcome new team members to your department.
2. Within the first week, make sure the new person conducts a Focus On You exercise with everyone on the team.
3. After you have implemented this new process for two new team members, reflect on what you have learned. How did it make them feel? How did it make the other team members feel?

ADJUST TO ACCOMMODATE NEW EMPLOYEES

As your career proceeds, you will sometimes find yourself with one or more new direct reports because (a) they are new hires or incoming transferees, or (b) you are the new manager of an existing team. In these cases, who should adjust to whom?

Many managers believe that their subordinates should do all (or almost all) the adjusting. That approach creates a relationship and a culture fundamentally based on power. How important will that make people feel? How likely is it they will perceive that manager as someone who cares about them? When managers base their influence on power rather than legitimacy, they create limitations on their own effectiveness, diminish employee loyalty, and undermine retention. That is not a great way to begin a relationship. And it is not the kind of culture the best managers create.

In the ideal culture, the manager and all team members should be open to making adjustments when people join the team in any capacity—whether they are new to the organization or transferring from another department. Blunt honesty about the company culture and the team culture help set the stage for this kind of willingness to adjust. As a manager, you should also do your best to clarify your own biases, values, expectations, and management style. These are the places in which, for very good reasons, you may be less willing or able to adjust. You should invite the same kind of blunt honesty from people you are selecting for your team. Where are their nonnegotiables, and where are they more willing and able to adjust? The more you share this type of information during the selection process, the easier it will be to understand how a candidate fits with the existing team. The better the fit, the more likely that everyone will be willing and able to adjust in ways that contribute to positive, synergistic working relationships.

LESSON

Intent is the most important element in these situations. Are you proactive in learning about your direct reports and open to them learning about you? Are you sincerely trying to make adjustments to improve your working relationships? If so, people will know it and appreciate it. In those situations in which things do not work out, they will know you sincerely tried to make the relationship work. Because you are a manager, your intent and your behavior have a substantial impact on your team's culture. When people see you behave this way consistently, they will behave this way, thus shaping a culture in which employees strive to adjust to better support one another.

EXPERIMENT: MAKE SOME ADJUSTMENTS

1. Identify one or more situations in which you are currently requiring employees to make all the adjustments for the relationship to work.
2. Change your approach and make some adjustments yourself.
3. Reflect on what happens to those relationships.

Chapter 48

CURATE YOUR ORGANIZATION'S FOLKLORE

E very human being is an unconscious cultural anthropologist. New employees learn the most about your culture through daily observation. They hear stories. They watch other people work. Every single day, they learn more about what gets celebrated and rewarded, what gets punished, and what gets ignored. *That*, ladies and gentlemen, is how people really learn the most about your culture. It is not at all helpful to new employees to mislead them about what your culture really is. It does not work. You cannot fool a good anthropologist.

LESSON

Employees can learn what you want them to learn about your company's culture during orientation. They learn what is true about your actual culture through stories and daily observation.

The stories people tell say a lot about an organization's culture. Stories stick. The backbone of history and culture, stories have been the vehicle for sharing information and transmitting values for millennia. What are the stories that get told and retold in your organization? They are the foundation for your organization's folklore. How can you leverage the power of stories to shape your organization's culture? Continually look for new stories, repeat old ones, and create platforms for telling and retelling the stories that exemplify and empower your organization's culture. Consider these examples:

The Engineer

In Chapter 25 we told the story about an engineer who restored a keynote speaker's videotape. That story became part of Ritz-Carlton's folklore.

The Housekeeper

In the course of cleaning a room, a Ritz-Carlton housekeeper noticed that the guest was almost out of an over-the-counter medicine he had been taking every day. She picked up a bottle of this medicine on her way to work the next day and left the bottle with a note saying that she had noticed he was almost out. The guest was genuinely touched that she had gone so far beyond cleaning his room and demonstrated such sincere caring about him as a person.

These stories say to employees, "This is who we are." When Larry worked for The Ritz-Carlton, almost everyone knew these stories. They were part of the company folklore. In a culture in which employees were encouraged to go outside their narrow job descriptions to fulfill even "the unexpressed wishes" (quotation from The Ritz-Carlton credo) of the guests, these stories brought that expectation to life. How much more powerful and inspiring are these stories compared to just saying, "We expect you to go the extra mile?" These moving stories tap into people's emotions, vividly communicate the organization's values and expectations, and specify exactly how those values can look in day-to-day work.

LESSON

Storytelling is *the* single most powerful method of shaping, teaching, and sustaining your culture.

EXPERIMENT: BUILD AN ARCHIVE OF STORIES

1. Watch and listen for stories that vividly illustrate your cultural values, beliefs, and expected behaviors.
2. Involve your employees in telling and collecting these stories.
3. Make it an ongoing practice rather than a one-time event.
4. Create opportunities to tell the stories often.
5. Make sure some sort of recognition occurs for the person who is the hero of the story.
6. After 90 days, reflect on what you have learned.

Chapter 49

ENLIVEN CULTURAL VALUES AND EXPECTATIONS

We have been using "culture" to refer to the shared values and beliefs of an organization and the full range of behaviors that are expected, valued, rewarded, punished, tolerated, or ignored. In addition to the overall organization culture, your department or team has its own culture. As a manager, you have the greatest influence on culture through your purposeful efforts to clearly describe your department's fundamental values and beliefs and the expected behaviors that go along with them.

Your team's values and beliefs must align with those of the larger organization, but the expected behaviors might be different. For example, if a cultural value is, "Pay close attention to detail," the behaviors expected of a grocery store cashier will be very different from the behaviors expected of a butcher who works in the same store. There will be different stories that best exemplify the values as they are lived out by people in different roles. Through the specific stories you tell, through your own behaviors, and through the rewards you provide, you must help your employees understand how the organization's values are expressed specifically in your department.

LESSON

Although your team's values and beliefs must align with the overall organization, the specific expected behaviors can vary from team to team.

Make sure you regularly and repeatedly communicate the expected behaviors for people on your team. You cannot just talk about this once. You must find a way to discuss it daily. How can you create a platform for that kind of regular communication and for the stories that make those values come alive?

Line Up

When Larry was with The Ritz-Carlton Hotel Company, every department, every shift met every day to discuss one of the 20 "basics" at the beginning of the shift. These were the most important values, beliefs, and behaviors that drove their success. Sometimes, people shared stories about times when they saw one of the basics in action. When the team had discussed number 20, they began again with number one. These daily meetings, known as "Line Up," took about 10 minutes. Line Up provided a platform for reenergizing people's commitment to these basics, and it created remarkable alignment among employees. It was a key strategy to The Ritz's success.

LESSON

Frequent, regular discussions about your organization's values, beliefs, and expected behaviors create alignment among employees and give every community member the opportunity to engage in both teaching and learning.

Furthermore, understand that discussion alone is not enough. As a manager, you must embody the values of the organization. Your example profoundly influences others. Remember that every employee is a cultural anthropologist. What you do is much more important than what you say. You must walk the talk.

LESSON

Discussion is not enough. As the manager, you must walk the talk.

Walking the talk goes beyond your own personal behavior, too. There is often a disconcerting incongruence between an organization's stated values and what it actually rewards. For example, an organization might say it values quality, but the tangible rewards go to people who are highly productive, even if their quality is not good. Take a brutally honest look at your formal and informal reward and punishment practices. To what degree are they aligned with your stated beliefs, values, and desired behaviors? You might need to change some practices to achieve better alignment, or you might wish to change some of the statements to more honestly tell it like it is.

LESSON

Ensure that your recognition and reward system, including performance evaluations and compensation reviews, actually rewards the right behaviors.

EXPERIMENT: CLARIFY AND ENLIVEN ORGANIZATION VALUES

1. Make sure you have translated your organization's values into specific behaviors relevant to your department. Make a list. Write them out.
2. Implement brief daily meetings (10 minutes) to review one of the items on your list. Discuss how that item is important to your success. Encourage discussion and stories from others.
3. When you have discussed the last item on the list, start again at the first item. People will have new experiences, examples, and stories to share. And the rhythm of repetition reinforces these values and behaviors.
4. Make sure that you recognize and reward employees who embody the items on the list.
5. After 90 days, reflect on what you have learned. Are you seeing more of the desired behaviors?

PROVIDE FREQUENT, CANDID FEEDBACK

Managers often ask how they can create a culture of feedback. Feedback is a tried and true mechanism for enhancing performance. What gets measured gets done. What gets measured *and rewarded* gets done better and more often (and more willingly). Ask yourself these questions about how you are providing feedback to the people you manage:

- How frequently do you provide feedback to the people on your team?
- Do they know what you expect?
- Do they know how they are doing?
- How long is the lag between their performance and your feedback?
- How do people feel about your feedback? Do they look forward to feedback from you or do they dread it?
- In your culture, is feedback a normal part of the regular routine, or is it a once a year occurrence?

Here is a story about how one manager made progress on creating a culture of feedback:

Frank and the Banquet Housemen

In large hotels, there is a team of employees known as banquet housemen whose job is to clean, set up, and tear down the hotel's many function rooms. It is a very physical job that involves moving tables and chairs in and out of storage areas, setting rooms to precise specifications, and cleaning

(continued)

197

(*continued*)

those rooms so that, when guests arrived, the room looks terrific down to the last detail. Banquet housemen, therefore, are deployed all over the hotel, and they work odd hours (so that guests can dance until 1:00 AM at their awards banquet, and some other group can start their meeting in that very same room at 8:00 AM).

Larry was the director of HR in a hotel where the banquet housemen team was suffering from low morale and high turnover. Leaders tried several interventions and strategies to improve the situation, but nothing worked. It came to pass that the supervisor left, and a guy named Frank was hired to replace him. Frank taught everyone in the hotel something about the power of feedback.

After about a week of assessing the situation, Frank created a short form performance evaluation. With a stack of these forms on a clipboard, he would randomly pop into a room where a couple of housemen were working. He would watch them work, and then he would complete an evaluation on each person and hand it to them. He did this every single day.

Within the first 30 days, turnover got even worse. But within 60 days, morale was very high, and turnover went to almost zero. The evaluations clarified Frank's expectations and provided individualized feedback so people knew exactly how they were measuring up to those expectations.

As he assessed the situation with his new team, Frank saw something that none of the other leaders in the hotel realized. There was no measurement system in place for housemen. Frank knew that feedback would improve performance, but he lacked a foundation for providing consistent, useful feedback. So he created one, and he demonstrated that building a culture of feedback has the potential to bring about serious improvements in performance, retention, and engagement.

LESSON

A measurement system is the absolute best way to provide objective and helpful feedback. For some jobs, it may be difficult to implement an objective measurement system. In those cases, frequent, candid feedback from a coach is a must—even though that feedback will be more subjective and perhaps less comparable across people.

These days, because almost everybody has a smartphone, it is easier to get feedback from end users. To evaluate banquet housemen today, we could ask meeting attendees or the meeting planner to answer one or two questions on their phones about the room setup. These ratings would evaluate performance, and they might even be better measurements than Frank's because they better reflect the end user experience. Of course, such measurements would have no impact on performance and culture if there were no mechanism for delivering the feedback to the individual housemen. Part of the genius of Frank's system was that it was immediate and individualized. The point here is that you do not need a fancy, complicated system. The simplest system that provides the most immediate, individualized feedback is best, as long as you fulfill one requirement: what you are measuring accurately reflects the extent to which people's work is meeting expectations and driving the right results.

When individuals or teams are given this kind of feedback on their performance, they are very likely to make adjustments on their own that lead to improved outcomes. But there are plenty of times when people do not know what to do differently to improve their scores. That is where managers need to go beyond just measuring and providing feedback to engage in actively coaching people on how they can perform better. Then, the measurement system will tell everyone how well that coaching worked. If you communicate clear expectations, implement a system to measure success, and provide frequent, candid feedback with effective coaching when needed, you will establish a feedback system that works.

Here are some underlying assumptions to all this that are important enough to mention, and that align with Ed Batista's *Harvard Business Review* article titled "Building a Feedback-Rich Culture" (Batista, 2013):[1]

1. Trust: The most effective feedback happens within positive, trust-based relationships. In the absence of that kind of trust, candid one-on-one feedback can backfire. And without high levels of trust among everyone on your team, you cannot hope to succeed at creating a culture of feedback. We have provided numerous ideas and suggestions for building trust and cultivating positive relationships in previous chapters. If trust is a question mark, we urge you to make that your top priority.

2. Normalcy: It seems to go without saying, but to create a culture of feedback, you must ensure that feedback becomes a regular part of what happens every day on your team. Also, if regular, candid feedback is not aligned with how your organization operates, you will be fighting an uphill battle. It is a battle worth fighting. Think about enlisting reinforcements from among your peers and leaders.

3. Personal Accountability: As we noted in the previous chapter, you have to walk the talk. If you want a culture of feedback, you have to be just as comfortable receiving feedback as you are giving it. And you have to create as much opportunity for feedback on your own performance as you create for feedback on your team's performance. You might even need to make a habit of asking for it.

4. Balance: Larry once heard a client say, "Around here continuous improvement means constant criticism." Feedback has to have some balance. Make sure you are not just focusing on misses and failures. Make sure you are also reviewing successes and high points, with the intent to figure out how to repeat those performances. This point is so important that the next chapter is devoted to it.

EXPERIMENT: EVALUATE YOUR FEEDBACK SYSTEM

1. Assess the current situation. Ask yourself these questions:
   a. How frequently do you provide feedback to the people on your team?
   b. Do they know what you expect?
   c. Do they know how they are doing?
   d. How long is the lag between their performance and your feedback?
   e. In your culture, is feedback a normal part of the routine, or is it a once a year occurrence?
   f. How do people feel about your feedback? Do they look forward to it or dread it?
2. Decide what to measure. If you do not have a feedback system in place, decide what metrics can give you a meaningful indication of how people are performing and decide how you will measure them.
3. If you have a feedback system in place, think about how effectively it measures what matters. Make any necessary changes.
4. Consider how your system addresses trust, normalcy, personal accountability, and balance.
5. Put your plan into action.
6. After 90 days, reflect on what you have learned. Has performance improved? Has morale improved? How have your answers to the list of questions in Step 1 on this list changed?

SHAPE A CULTURE OF RECOGNITION AND APPRECIATION

In many organizations, out of a sincere effort to improve performance, instances of criticism and negative feedback (discussions about what is wrong) far outnumber instances of positive feedback. But as Theodore Roosevelt said, "It is not the critic who counts." Monday morning quarterbacking is so much easier than standing on the field and making great plays happen in real time. You can probably think of stories to illustrate that idea. Larry has one too:

What Larry Learned at Cornell

I was one of about 25 hospitality industry executives who attended a board of advisors meeting at Cornell University. Cornell has a highly regarded four-year program to prepare students for careers in the hotel industry. Every member of this advisory board had a sincere desire to improve both the university's program and the industry's ability to serve its customers. They were committed to constructive collaboration to achieve these goals.

Several professors delivered presentations about industry research projects they had recently completed or had under way. The board members asked questions, took part in discussions, and were otherwise engaged. But after the presentations, board members expressed disappointment that the

(continued)

(*continued*)

school's research projects had little relevance and practical value to people actually doing business in the industry.

The board then discussed various strategies to ensure that future research would be more relevant. One person suggested that a subcommittee of the board could review proposed research projects and issue opinions about relevance. The issue of academic freedom came up, and it became clear that the kind of research projects that helped the careers of professors frequently were not the kind that industry executives would consider relevant and practical.

Then something interesting happened. The conference leader asked the board members what kinds of research projects *would* be relevant, practical, and helpful to industry executives.

Cue sound of crickets chirping.

Perhaps it is not so easy to identify relevant research topics in this industry.

After some moments of silence, one board member offered five ideas, but there was not a high degree of enthusiasm for any of them. Not one other board member offered an idea—including the two or three people who had been most vocal in their criticism about the relevancy of the professors' research.

LESSON

As managers, we have to do more than criticize. We have to actually help. If we cannot offer any coaching, ideas, resources, alternatives, or other forms of meaningful help to those in whom we are disappointed, then we should quit criticizing people for not doing better.

As a manager, move beyond just criticizing to actually helping, and go one step further. Promote a culture of recognition and appreciation. Unfortunately, the natural wiring of our brains makes this quite challenging. Our brains are hardwired to detect threats and other kinds of problems. This wiring has great survival value. Our natural tendency to focus on what is wrong and to give more weight to negative information than to positive information has been well documented by research psychologists. Rozin and Royzman[1] sum it up with the old adage, "A spoonful of tar can spoil a barrel of honey, but a spoonful of honey does nothing for a barrel of tar." Baumeister et al.[2] say it all in the title of their extensive literature review: Bad Is Stronger than Good. The negative bias goes right down to human neurobiology, where the natural high of a dopamine rush wears off after only a couple of hours, while the effects of the stress hormone cortisol last up to 24 hours.[3] Too often, people focus so much on the negative that they forget to acknowledge their successes. Here is a story from Larry that clearly illustrates that point:

I Made My Budget!

In 2009, I was visiting a client, which was a resort in the Caribbean. Travel to the islands was way down, and the resort business was really hurting. On the first day of my assignment, I had breakfast with the general manager to clarify his expectations for my visit. His mood was not upbeat.

When I asked him to tell me about a success he had recently, he was unable to think of anything. So we moved on in our conversation. About 20 minutes into this meeting he blurted out, "I made budget last month!"

At this particular time, making budget was extremely difficult. That counted as a ringing success. But it took him 20 minutes to think of it. That is because we spend so much time focusing on problems.

LESSON

Even during difficult, challenging times, people achieve successes, but we often barely acknowledge them because we are so focused on what is wrong. Because of the "wiring" of our brains, we have to be more intentional in helping our people acknowledge and celebrate successes. It adds more positivity to the environment.

Shape a culture that has the potential to overpower the built-in negative bias. Increase your focus on successes and high points, and encourage others to do so as well. You will increase your positive influence and bring about noticeable change. People will have more spring in their step, a more positive attitude, and a higher level of motivation and engagement. Your mood will improve as well, because you will learn about successes that otherwise would not have come to your attention.

EXPERIMENT: INTENTIONALLY FOCUS ON SUCCESS

1. Begin every meeting by asking each person to briefly mention a recent success or high point they have had. Make this a habit. No exceptions. Build it into the agenda.
2. After 90 days, reflect on what you have learned. How did people react to learning about others' successes? How did this change the tone of the meetings? Have other managers or teams adopted this practice?

Nurturing a culture of recognition and appreciation is more impactful than implementing specific recognition programs. Improving the ratio of positive to negative feedback (praise versus criticism) will enhance your ability to make a difference in your employees' lives and improve your business results. The positive to negative ratio (sometimes called the Gottman Ratio or the Losada Ratio) has been extensively researched. Despite some academic arguments about the best mathematical approach to understanding the ratio, Fredrickson[4] argues convincingly that the preponderance of evidence points toward an ideal ratio of somewhere between 3:1 and 5:1 of positive to negative—and that we should avoid throwing out the baby with the mathematical bathwater. This is the ratio that separates high-performing teams from moderately or poorly performing ones.[5] It is also the ratio that separates stable marriages from those that are much more likely to end in divorce.[6] Researchers are clear that negative feedback has value at times; the ratio is not 3:0, after all. However, because our brains give more weight to bad rather than good, a 1:1 ratio is never optimal.

What does all this mean in practical terms? Sandwiching criticism with praise is not enough. That only gets you a 2:1 ratio. Besides the ratio, the fact that criticism is mixed in with praise activates the negative bias; it is almost a sure bet that the praise will be quickly forgotten and dismissed as the criticism steals the show. To optimize performance, engagement, and retention, you will want to hit that 3:1 to 5:1 ratio, and the likelihood of being able to hit that ratio increases if you create a culture in which positive feedback is the norm so that people on your team can provide it to each other with the same intention that drives you to provide positive feedback to them.

Because of our natural tendency to focus on the negative, appreciative cultures are rare, but their benefits are significant. Consider a few statistics:[7]

- People are less likely to express gratitude at work than almost anywhere else.
- Only 10 percent of people express appreciation to their coworkers on a daily basis.

- A full 60 percent never say thank you or express gratitude at work, or do it only once or twice a year.
- At the same time, 81 percent say they would work harder for a more grateful manager.

How much harder do you think those 81 percent of the people would work for a more grateful manager? Another study suggests they will work about 50 percent harder.[8] In a field experiment with fundraisers working for a university, the director visited with some (but not all) workers, thanking them for their hard work and the contributions they were making to the university. After being thanked, that group of workers made 50 percent more phone calls compared to the previous week. The workers who were not thanked for their work made about the same number of calls as they did in the previous week. What kind of impact would it make on your business if people were 50 percent more productive?

Given the difference an appreciative culture can make in performance, this statistic from another study is sobering: 83 percent of employees reported that their organizations' cultures do not strongly support recognition. This matches eerily well with the 87 percent of organizations reporting that they have recognition programs designed primarily to recognize tenure and service and suggests that, in the minds of employees, recognition for tenure "doesn't count."

There are some big disconnects between what leaders think is happening in organizations and what employees are actually experiencing, too. In the same study, 80 percent of senior leaders thought their employees were being recognized at least monthly, but only 22 percent of individual contributors reported that they were being recognized that often.[9]

LESSON

Implement formal recognition programs, but don't stop there. Nurture an appreciative culture through your daily interactions. There are no secrets about what to do or how to do it. You just have to do it.

In cultivating an appreciative culture, you should focus primarily on the center of your circle of influence—your own behavior. Make a personal commitment to express appreciation more frequently. Here are some easy, inexpensive ways to do this:

- Say, "Thank you," more often. Say it with sincerity. What could be easier? After all these years, this is still number one, and it can improve performance by as much as 50 percent.

- Write a handwritten note. This takes about three minutes, on average, and these are so valued that people save them.
- Walk a person into your supervisor's office and tell your supervisor what he or she did that was so great.
- Write a note and mail it to his or her home, so the family can read it, too.
- Write a note to someone's parents or spouse. This is so unusual it really makes an impression.
- Invest some one-on-one time with a top performer. Take him or her out for a cup of coffee, and explain why you are doing it.
- If, *and only if*, the person likes public recognition, give him or her a round of applause.
- Send cards to your direct reports on important days like birthdays, anniversaries, graduations, and so forth.
- Go out after work or at lunch to informally celebrate individual or team successes.

EXPERIMENT: CULTIVATE AN APPRECIATIVE CULTURE

1. Select three items from the preceding list.
2. Commit to doing those three things more frequently and more consistently for 90 days.
3. Reflect on what you have learned. How did it make you feel? How did it make others feel? Have you noticed other people doing more of those things?

The next chapter describes "emotional rehiring," which is another powerful strategy for appreciating and recognizing people—so powerful, in fact, that we are giving it its own chapter. But we want to share one important caveat with you now. We hinted at it in the preceding list of ideas, and it bears further emphasis. In the process of providing meaningful positive feedback, it is critical that you individualize. What is positive to one person can be negative to another. Here is another story from Larry to illustrate:

Alexis's Million Dollar Group

When I was general manager of The Ritz-Carlton, Tysons Corner, Alexis, a sales associate, booked and hosted a small group of very wealthy guests for an extended stay in our hotel. When they checked out, the bill was more than 1 million dollars. This was an unprecedented accomplishment worthy of a significant gesture of recognition. Every employee received a monetary bonus for this, and Alexis was particularly deserving of special recognition.

We knew Alexis had a thing for Hermès scarfs, so we bought her Hermès' latest offering. We had the check from the guest photocopied and framed. We also cut her a very large bonus check. I presented her with these items at our weekly staff meeting, which was attended by all of the managers. She graciously accepted and received a well-deserved standing ovation.

Immediately after the staff meeting, she was in my office. "Please don't do that again," she said, "I really don't like being singled out in public like that. I would much prefer if you came to my office and did it quietly and personally."

LESSON

The best forms of recognition are individualized to the person. If you are buying a gift, buy something related to that individual's personal interests and values. And make sure the process of presenting the recognition is also individualized.

EXPERIMENT: INDIVIDUALIZED RECOGNITION

1. Ask each of your direct reports the following questions and take notes:
   a. What contributions or successes do you want to be recognized for?
   b. When you accomplish something worthy of recognition, who do you want to know it?
   c. What is the best gesture of recognition you have ever received? Why was it the best?
   d. What form of recognition is most meaningful to you?

(*continued*)

(*continued*)

2. Act on what you heard. When someone has earned a gesture of recognition, consult your notes and give them something individualized to their interests.

3. After you have done this three times, reflect on what you have learned. How did it make the recipients feel? How did it make you feel? Have others adopted this practice?

EMOTIONALLY REHIRE PEOPLE

E motional rehiring is a simple but powerful form of positive feedback. It is as simple as authentically telling someone why you are thankful to have him or her on your team. It is easy to do, and if you make this simple practice a common part of your culture, you will increase appreciation, build loyalty, and enhance engagement.

Emotional rehiring can be done in a conversation or in writing. In a conversation, it takes less than 30 seconds. Writing the same message might take you all of three or four minutes and creates a tangible, permanent token of your appreciation. This tiny investment of effort can deliver enormous returns over time.

Here is an example of what emotional rehiring might look like in writing:

Bruno,
Congratulations on earning an important referral from our new client. Sponta-
neous referrals are the highest form of praise. Your ability to listen, your sense of
urgency, and your unwavering dedication to delivering the highest quality are
building our business. I'm glad you're here!
Larry

This is a major deposit in Bruno's emotional bank account. Note that it highlights a specific accomplishment, calls attention to three specific strengths, and points out the contribution to the organization. The last sentence is the punch line. It explicitly rehires the person. Predictably, this works only if it is completely authentic.

Here are some guidelines to help you maximize its impact:

1. Refer to a specific example of what the person did.
2. State clearly how it makes a difference, adds value, or contributes to the mission.
3. Use a phrase that expresses the sentiment, "I'm glad you're here."
4. Put it in an envelope to create some anticipation.
5. Give it to the person.

How would you feel if your boss did this for you from time to time? If you make this a part of your culture, you will also improve the emotional hygiene of your organization, you will increase the ratio of positive to negative comments, and some people may even follow your lead and start doing this themselves.

You can do this for people who do not report to you and for people who are not part of your organization like clients or vendors. You can also extend this as a powerful form of positive feedback to your friends and family members.

Within your organization, do you think a week goes by without someone doing something worthy of recognition or appreciation? (Hint: The correct answer is, "No.")

What if you wrote at least one note every week? What if every person in management in your organization wrote one a week? How many tangible instances of appreciation or recognition would you generate in a year?

Someone always asks, "Can you overdo this?" That should be your problem. Remember the optimal positive to negative ratio is somewhere between 3:1 and 5:1. Remember bad is stronger than good. Remember that people hear plenty of criticism. Be the one person who catches people doing things right and recognizes them for it. You really cannot overdo positive feedback. The only potential pitfall is sincerity. If each note is sincere and specific, and highlights something meaningful, you can't overdo this kind of positive feedback, especially when it ends with the, "I'm glad you're here," kind of sentiment that creates an emotional rehire. However, if you can't be sincere and authentic, better not do it at all.

You might think you do not have the time to do this. Based on data from our training programs that use this as an exercise, if you already have the notecard and a pen, the average amount of time to write a note that emotionally rehires someone is three to four minutes. Why wouldn't you be willing to invest three to four minutes a week on a strategy that will improve morale, engagement, and job satisfaction? Why wouldn't you invest three to four minutes a week to make a greater difference as a manager?

LESSON

Emotional rehiring is a big deal. There are very few practices that cost less money, take less time, and contribute more to retention and engagement.

EXPERIMENT: EMOTIONAL REHIRING

1. Write three notes of appreciation or affirmation every week for the next month. This should take you about 15 minutes total each week.
2. Write a physical note on a card. That means more than email.
3. When you write a note, highlight something specific the person has done.
4. Conclude the note with the phrase: "I'm glad you're here," or, "I'm glad you're part of our team," or another sincere expression that seals the deal on the emotional rehiring.
5. Remember, you do not have to limit these notes to the people you manage or even to people at work.
6. At the end of the month, reflect on what you have learned. How did writing the notes make you feel? How did it make others feel?
7. Extra credit: At least once during the month, instead of writing the note to the person, write it to the person's parents or spouse. Do not mention it to the person. Just mail it to his or her parents or spouse.

Thanksgiving presents a wonderful opportunity to emotionally rehire people who are important to you—in both your personal and professional lives. Consider sending Thanksgiving cards instead of Christmas cards or generic holiday cards. This is a specific application of emotional rehiring.

The sheer number of cards sent around the Christmas season makes it impossible for your card to stand out. But if you send Thanksgiving cards, they arrive earlier than others and you do not have to worry about the person's religion. Give it a try.

EXPERIMENT: THANKSGIVING CARDS

1. This year write a Thanksgiving card to each member of your team.
2. Tell the person something specific about him or her for which you are thankful.
3. Mail these cards to each person's home.
4. See what kind of response you get.
5. Extra credit: Do this with your best customers.

CELEBRATE PERSONAL AND PROFESSIONAL ACCOMPLISHMENTS

In addition to showing appreciation one-on-one, engage in group celebrations to mark personal and professional achievements. In every organization, some accomplishments receive company-sponsored celebrations and others are left to informal celebrations not on company time. Don't worry about whether something is company sponsored. The important thing is to celebrate.

LESSON

Building a celebratory culture increases motivation and engagement, enhances relationships, and translates directly into improved productivity. Celebrations should occur as chronologically close to the events as possible.

Significant occasions often involve ceremony. One purpose of ceremony is to convey that something important is happening. The more important the event, the more ceremony is involved. Think about the ceremony around weddings, inaugurations, and graduations. We encourage you to think about the significance of what you are celebrating. The more significant the event, the more ceremony you create.

As a manager, what is your obligation? You work in an established culture in which certain achievements and milestones are always the occasion for a company-sanctioned celebration, with well-established norms for the degree of

213

ceremony considered appropriate. We advise you to comply with those cultural norms.

For those achievements and milestones that do not merit officially sanctioned celebrations, you, the manager, should ensure that some informal celebration occurs. The type of celebration is less important than the fact that the achievement or milestone is sincerely acknowledged. It can be milk and cookies. A round of applause. Flowers. Singing, "Happy Birthday." Gathering after work. It does not have to be expensive or time consuming. But it does have to be sincere.

EXPERIMENT: CELEBRATE MILESTONES

1. Identify some events you do not currently celebrate, such as birthdays, graduations, engagements, and so on.
2. If you are not good at organizing these types of events, tap someone on your team who enjoys it.
3. Begin celebrating these events on a regular basis. Remember, it does not have to be expensive. Do things that everyone on the team can afford.
4. After six months, reflect on how this has affected your team. What has changed about these celebrations since you started?

ASK, "HOW CAN I HELP?"

This question is a deeply ingrained part of the culture of our company, Talent Plus. We take no credit for it. It arises from the character of our founders, who care deeply for each and every associate. Because of their model, when any associate experiences a challenge in his or her professional or personal life, the immediate response from everyone is, "How can I help?"

The power in, "How can I help," goes beyond simply asking the question and resides in the genuine commitment to extend ourselves to help one another. In our culture, caring is not just a feeling. In our culture, caring demands action. We go to extraordinary lengths to support one another during challenging times. We make sure our associates' job responsibilities are covered. We ensure they know they can take the time they need to deal with their challenges. On the personal side, we have seen associates cook meals, babysit children, give rides to the doctor, mow lawns, and clean houses—just to cite a few examples. It is one of the things we value most about our culture.

Larry has been on the receiving end of this practice. Here is a brief story.

Family Emergency

Some years ago, I had a family emergency that required my wife and I to start driving immediately from Lincoln, Nebraska, to Tucson, Arizona—a 24-hour drive. After we started driving (at 9:00 PM), I left messages with several people about what was going on. About 12 hours later, my boss, Kimberly Rath (one of the founders) called me. She did not ask how long I would be gone. She did not ask about the status of my work responsibilities. She just asked, "How can I help?"

LESSON

In these times, thought leaders are focusing on engagement. We are investing huge resources in surveys and action plans. But we should not overlook simple, effective strategies that demonstrate to people that they are significant as human beings and that we truly care. The question, "How can I help?" when asked sincerely, has enormous power.

If you are part of a culture that lives this value, we hope you appreciate it. If you are not in that type of culture, you can start a positive change. You can start asking this question with the people who report to you, and you can teach them to ask the question as well. You will increase your positive influence in their lives and in your organization. That is the definition of managing to make a difference.

EXPERIMENT: ASK, "HOW CAN I HELP?"

1. When people come to you with a challenge or problem, whether in their professional or personal life, first listen to understand.
2. Then ask this question: "How can I help?" (and mean it—be prepared to deliver on anything they share that would be helpful).
3. Do this for 90 days.
4. Reflect on what you have learned. How did this question change the nature of those interactions?

Chapter 55

ENCOURAGE EMPLOYEES TO HAVE FUN

In these times, having fun must be part of your culture. Employees expect to be able to have fun at work. When employees take a little time from their work to have some fun, it might look like wasted time, but it is a great investment. When people have fun together, relationships are improved. A fun work environment also makes a team or organization more attractive to prospective employees. Among college-age job seekers (those millennials who are all the buzz), workplace fun is an even stronger predictor of a company's attractiveness than compensation or opportunities for advancement.[1] Fun generally improves retention, engagement, and productivity, though researchers caution managers to strike the right balance between fun and a focus on high performance.[2] We realize this insight is not news to anyone, but we felt we could not ignore a topic as fundamental as fun in a section titled "Shape Your Culture."

LESSON

Encouraging employees to have fun at work while maintaining a focus on high performance builds closer relationships, improves engagement, and increases productivity.

As you know, there are all kinds of ways for people to have fun. In our company, for example, many people are avid sports fans. When the big game is on, we set up a large function room for group viewing. People bring their computers and work while they watch the game together. We even provide snacks. We do a lot of other fun things as well, but we certainly do not have a monopoly on how to have fun. There are plenty of ideas out there.

Even if you are not good at making work fun, you can manage in a way that makes fun part of your culture. Find the people on your staff who are good at it, and let them take the lead.

EXPERIMENT: INCREASE THE FUN

1. Ask your people for their ideas about how to have more fun at work.
2. Ask your friends how their organizations make the workplace more fun.
3. Implement some of these ideas.
4. After 90 days, reflect on what you have learned. How has this affected engagement? Productivity? Relationships?

ADDRESS POOR PERFORMANCE

As much as people value fun, they know they have a job to do, and they want a manager who balances fun with a focus on performance. Top performers thrive in a culture of clear expectations and accountability. Confident in their capabilities, they are motivated by challenges that require them to stretch and by goals that are difficult to achieve. They want to know their supervisor believes they are capable of achieving goals that others cannot. They also crave the intrinsic satisfaction experienced when they attain those goals. In fact, some top performers thrive on doing things others say can't be done. The more clarity you can bring to expectations, the easier it is for everyone. Ideally, there are objective metrics attached to the expectations you set so that, as a manager, you can hold people accountable for meeting them and provide recognition and rewards when they do. Recognize that top performers expect you both to reward people who meet and exceed performance expectations and to address poor performance with people who fail to meet those same expectations.

If your goal is managing to make a difference, start by establishing clear goals and choosing the right metrics to assess performance. Answer these questions:

1. "If X is performing with excellence in this role, how will we know it?"
2. "What will we see happening? What will we not see happening?"

Sometimes identifying the right metrics is difficult. In the absence of metrics, the person must rely solely on your qualitative feedback as a manager. Whether you have metrics or must rely on more subjective assessments, make sure you are giving people frequent, candid feedback about their performance.

Accountability must be accompanied by empowerment. If you are going to hold people accountable for meeting certain expectations, you must allow them to decide how they will go about achieving those results. If an employee or a team is merely carrying out your directions about the *how*, you are the owner of the results, not them, and you cannot legitimately hold them accountable for those results. Make sure you empower people to the same extent you want to hold them accountable for results.

When you have the metrics, feedback, empowerment, and accountability right, poor performance becomes obvious. In most cases of poor performance, the employee knows that there is a problem even before you do. It is not kind or helpful to leave someone in a situation in which he or she is failing. Everyone knows there is a performance problem. You know there is a performance problem. And in many cases, everyone on the team knows there is a performance problem because they are picking up the slack in some way. Your team members and especially your top performers want you to address it. Performance matters to them. They will lose respect for you as a manager if you do not deal with poor performance.

Determining the consequences for poor performance is not always straightforward. Consequences must be tailored to suit the situation. Managers can easily err on both sides of this issue. This is where some art comes in. If you continue to accept excuses for not meeting expectations, you wind up carrying unproductive people, thereby negatively affecting your customers, your employees, and your company. On the other hand, everyone screws up from time to time. If you react too harshly, you can lose an employee who can add a great deal of value over time. When you are addressing poor performance, all of your employees are watching. They will correctly conclude that you will deal with them similarly if they find themselves in a similar situation. Be thoughtful about what message you are sending, but do not blindly follow policies and procedures or respond in exactly the same way to every situation.

The root cause for each instance of failure must be considered. Here are some questions you can ask that might help you understand why poor performance exists, so you can address it in the most effective ways:

1. Did the employee fail to put in enough effort?
2. Did he or she have the right training and resources?
3. Did the employee know what was expected?
4. Do the expectations align with the employee's strengths?
5. When this person encountered a problem, did he or she bring it to someone's attention and seek help?
6. Is this failure an anomaly or is this a well-established pattern?
7. Was there an unforeseeable event that had a material impact on this person's ability to achieve the goals?

It is important to hold people accountable. But it is also important to ensure that the consequences are thoughtfully tailored to each situation.

LESSON

Your employees expect you to hold people accountable. The way you respond to poor performance must be thoughtfully tailored to each situation.

EXPERIMENT: ADDRESS POOR PERFORMANCE

1. Discuss poor performance one-on-one, privately.
2. State the facts (metrics, observed behaviors) and compare those to established goals or expectations.
3. Make it clear that your goal is to help the person improve.
4. Focus the dialogue on identifying the root causes for the poor performance. Collaborate about ways to address those causes.
5. Restate expectations and agree on when to review this situation again (30 days? 90 days?).
6. Be clear about the consequences of not improving.
7. If you commit to doing something to help this person, make absolutely sure you deliver.
8. Hold him or her accountable to improve. If you and the person cannot improve the performance, you must take the action you think suits the situation.

Chapter 57

ADDRESS BAD BEHAVIOR

This chapter is related to the previous chapter, but the focus is on bad (undesirable, inappropriate, unethical, or immoral) behavior rather than on poor performance. This may seem like a very straightforward topic at first. You may be thinking, "Larry and Kim, this is not even worthy of discussion. Bad behavior should be punished. End of story." It turns out to be a much more challenging topic than it might appear because you, as a manager, have to answer two questions:

1. Just how bad was the behavior? Was it a violation of etiquette or ethics?
2. What should the consequences be?

First, it is important to understand that what counts as bad behavior in one culture might well be characterized as perfectly acceptable in another. For example, in some organizations, being late to meetings is considered disrespectful toward the other participants, and therefore "bad behavior" of the variety that is considered rude, but not unethical. In other organizations, not being on time to meetings is the norm. It is routinely tolerated and, therefore, not even a violation of etiquette.

As we have said, it is vitally important to understand that the stated values of the organization are not the actual values. Every employee is a natural cultural anthropologist who learns the actual values of an organization by observation.

1. What behaviors are rewarded?
2. What behaviors are condemned and punished?
3. What behaviors are ignored?

Ultimately managers and leaders, through their action or inaction, determine the organization's official answers to these questions, no matter what is written or formally stated.

To further complicate matters, it is also important to understand that all of this is a moving target. The answers to these questions evolve over time. In every community of people, there is frequent discussion—judgmental discussion— about the behavior of others. This is how a community confirms and adjusts its written and unwritten code of behavior. Right now, for example, our standards for the use of mobile devices and computers in meetings is in flux. Is it rude to check emails and texts during a meeting? Is it okay in some meetings, but not in others? In situations in which it is not okay, how should the organization respond?

As a manager, you are accountable to determine the final answers to these questions in your department. It is sometimes a struggle to arrive at the answer that is appropriate for each individual situation. This is difficult. We would likely tolerate our number one salesperson being late to meetings even if our culture labeled that behavior as disrespectful. But we would not tolerate disrespect in the form of racial slurs. Somewhere between those two situations there is a line, but we cannot tell you exactly where it is.

No matter where the line is, there are some behaviors that should be treated with zero tolerance. Recently in the United States, we have seen situations in which egregious behaviors have become institutionalized. Here are some examples. In certain organizations, rapes are not properly investigated, nor are the rapists held accountable. Known product defects causing injury, illness, and death are intentionally covered up. Corners are cut on safety practices to reduce costs. Child abuse and domestic abuse are tolerated, and known abusers are not held accountable. Bribery is tolerated to achieve business goals. Stealing from customers is encouraged to achieve sales goals.

LESSON

Institutionalized bad behaviors can only occur in a culture in which the managers and leaders have somehow established that those behaviors are okay. If unethical or immoral behaviors are routinely occurring under your watch, it is your fault. Even if you are not aware of the actual behaviors, you have somehow communicated that they are okay.

Greater oversight is not the answer to reducing bad behavior. As a manager, you should be proactive. You should make honesty and integrity absolute tickets to admission for all employees and nonnegotiable conditions of continuing employment. You should make strong and clear statements about the organization's commitment to doing the right things right. You should walk your talk. When someone exhibits unethical or immoral behaviors, you should take swift and unequivocal action to hold him or her accountable. Zero tolerance. You should make it easy and safe for people to blow the whistle, and you should reward people who shine the light on unethical or dishonest behavior.

Here is an example of how easily dishonesty can creep into a culture. Many organizations require a doctor's note for certain absences. Every employee knows where they can get a doctor's note. When an employee needs a day off for some reason (but is not sick), he or she brings in a note. You know no one was sick. He or she knows you know, and you have just condoned dishonesty in this situation. It is a slippery slope. It becomes easier to condone the next deception. Trust is eroded, and this generates more dysfunctional behavior.

How would this look different if you just gave the employee the day off, without requiring this sham? You might not have the authority to change this now, but someday you will have that authority. We hope you remember this discussion. You can shape a healthier culture.

There is no experiment in this chapter. Experimenting is inappropriate on matters of ethics and morals.

To minimize bad behavior, select people with impeccable honesty and integrity. Clarify what behaviors are acceptable and unacceptable. Tailor the consequences of unacceptable behavior to the person and the situation. Clarify what behaviors are in the zero-tolerance zone, and respond rapidly when people behave in those ways. Finally, reward those who bring bad behavior to light. Remember that what you do speaks louder than what you say. If you do this effectively, bad behavior will occur occasionally, but it will not become institutionalized.

EXERT MORAL AUTHORITY

M anaging to make a difference involves creating a culture that encourages people to become their best selves. As a manager, there are a number of ways you can help employees pursue this noble goal. You can recognize and reward people for exemplary behavior. You can punish people for unacceptable behavior. But the most powerful strategy is to exert moral authority.

The Surgeon General

Dr. C. Everett Koop was an American hero. Among his numerous accomplishments, as Surgeon General of the United States, he issued eight reports about the dangers of smoking and required tobacco companies to print health warnings on cigarette packages. We take these things for granted today, but at the time, his courageous stance was revolutionary and controversial.

During the early days of his antismoking campaign, he appeared on the *Tonight Show*, and Johnny Carson asked the following question: "When you arrive at a party, when you walk in the door, do people quickly put out their cigarettes?" Smiling, he replied, "Yes, they do."

That, ladies and gentlemen, is moral authority. It does not arise from power or title. When a manager exerts moral authority, people behave better in his or her presence. And they do so not because they fear punishment or seek reward. They do so simply because the manager's mere presence inspires them.

Moral authority includes integrity, but it is much more. One can act with integrity, but not be kind. One can be scrupulously honest, but not be generous. To exert moral authority, one must be the kind of person others look up to and want to emulate.

227

LESSON

When you exert moral authority, your capacity to influence others increases dramatically, thus improving your ability to help them grow as human beings. This is one of the most powerful ways to shape a culture.

How do you exert moral authority?

Epitomize the values you espouse. Walk your talk. This maxim has come up in multiple places in this book because it is so central to managing to make a difference. Who you are speaks more loudly than what you say. Failure to walk your talk will earn you a well-deserved reputation for hypocrisy. Think about politicians who forcefully espouse family values while committing adultery. Disgusting. Who wants to follow a hypocrite?

Walking your talk is easy when the weather is good. But do you adhere to your stated principles when it is difficult, when doing so costs you in some way? Do all of your decisions and actions build your moral authority—everything from the big decisions about your business to the small actions (or inactions) in your daily interactions? The more consistently you exemplify the character traits and behaviors you espouse, the more likely you will earn—and exert—moral authority.

Your reputation is built by your decisions and actions as you move through life. Doing the right thing is easy when it is convenient and painless. But what about when it is not?

- What do you do when "the right thing" is not at all clear?
- What do you do when it is inconvenient and likely to cause you some pain?
- What do you do when you have done something wrong?

Discuss the alternatives. The right thing to do is not always clear. The world does not fit neatly into the categories we create. Vigorous, candid discussion is healthy. And well-meaning, intelligent people can disagree. Discussing alternatives transparently creates a powerful demonstration that you are willing to ask hard questions and that you are striving to find the right answers. Ultimately, however, you must act. Not everyone will agree with your point of view. When you have to make these types of decisions, ask yourself, "Am I comfortable explaining this decision in a public forum?" If not, find a different course of action.

Avoid even the appearance of impropriety. A senior partner taught Larry this when he was practicing law. It is not enough to know you are doing the right thing. You must be aware of how others might see it. The appearance of impropriety often causes huge damage even if one's innocence is later established. At the very least, it tarnishes your reputation. If something will look wrong even though is not, choose not to do it. If you are called upon to explain why you have done something, you have already made a mistake.

Operate with transparency. As our friend and colleague, Bill Kerrey, says, "Sunshine disinfects." Mysteries breed suspicion. Transparency is the best way to avoid the appearance of impropriety.

Don't do something just because you can get away with it. Temptation is all around us. Giving in to temptation can bring heavy costs. Volkswagen's culture of cheating on emissions tests cost the company billions of dollars. Wells Fargo's culture of defrauding customers put more than 5,000 employees out of work. In many cases, a manager can do things that are not right because nobody has the power to hold him or her accountable. This is how bullying, sexual harassment, and other abuses of power arise. A company president who forbids HR to record her vacation time invites people to wonder, "What else is she getting away with?"

If you do things just because you can get away with them, you not only create suspicion; you also set an example that others are likely to emulate. You will create a culture that makes it okay for people to see what they can get away with. No ethics, no integrity, no honor, no trust. As a manager, don't do this and don't condone it when you find others doing it.

Admit your mistakes, apologize, and do your best to make things right. We have written about this earlier in the book, but it bears repeating here. Too many managers think it is a sign of weakness to admit a mistake. On the contrary, it is a sign of strength. Who in their right mind believes their manager is incapable of error? Managers who do not admit mistakes undermine their moral authority.

Adhere to your principles even when it is difficult, costly, and painful. We have shining examples of this. To name just a few: Mohandas Gandhi; Abraham Lincoln; Socrates; Nelson Mandela; the demonstrators in Tiananmen Square; Dr. Martin Luther King, Jr.; the protesters who crossed the Edmund Pettus Bridge in Selma; and Rosa Parks. You can add your own examples to the list. These kinds of role models inspire people to action through their moral authority. We would all do well to emulate their example.

EXPERIMENT: INCREASE YOUR MORAL AUTHORITY

1. Review the previous statements in italics. We restate them here for your convenience.
   a. Epitomize the values you espouse. Walk your talk.
   b. Discuss the alternatives.
   c. Avoid even the appearance of impropriety.
   d. Don't do something just because you can get away with it.

(continued)

(*continued*)

    e. Admit your mistakes, apologize, and do your best to make things right.

    f. Adhere to your principles even when it is difficult, costly, and painful.

2. Rate your own behavior on each item, using a 1 to 10 scale, with 1 indicating poor and 10 indicating excellent.

3. For the item you rated highest, reflect on how it has affected your moral authority and think about whether and how you see people on your team embracing it as a cultural value.

4. For the item you rated lowest, ask the following questions:

    a. If I were to rate myself a 10 on that item, what would I see happening? What would I see not happening?

    b. What do I need to do differently to improve my rating?

5. When you are satisfied with your improvement on that item, pick another one to work on.

6. After six months, reflect on what you have learned. How do others feel about you? How do you feel when you look in the mirror?

Research has established that the impact of moral authority on organization culture extends beyond your personal experience as a manager. It drives measurable business results.[1] Economist Luigi Guiso and his colleagues analyzed data from 385 firms. The vast majority of those firms advertised values on their websites related to integrity, but those advertised values had no impact on business results. What did influence business results were employees' perceptions of management integrity to those cultural values.

They studied workers' ratings on two statements related to management integrity:

1. Management's actions match its words.
2. Management is honest and ethical in its business practices.

Higher levels of perceived integrity based on those statements were correlated with better business outcomes—higher productivity and profitability, better industrial relations (less unionization), and greater attractiveness to potential job applicants.

As a manager and leader, you are "management" in the eyes of your organization's employees. Your moral authority drives their perceptions not just of you as an individual but of your company's culture and its management as a whole. Those perceptions connect to measurable business outcomes.

Chapter 59

RISE ABOVE THE POLITICS

If you have two or more human beings in a community, you are going to have politics. In your organization's culture, politics may play a greater or lesser role. But it is almost inevitable that, because of politics, some people will be favored with power, influence, and rewards they did not earn. As many astute thinkers have pointed out, organization politics are a fact of life. So don't bemoan reality. Accept it and deal with it.

Based on that reality, you can make one of two choices. You can make the decision to gain power by devoting your time to politics. If that is your choice, we refer you to *The Prince* by Niccolò Machiavelli. Alternatively, you can also make the decision to rise above the politics and devote your time to creating value. If you choose the latter, doing the following seven things will ensure that you rise above the politics.

Deliver Exemplary Performance   First and foremost deliver results that exceed expectations. If nepotism, sycophantism, or other forms of favoritism mean more than outstanding performance in your organization, the organization is doomed to mediocrity or worse. The culture will be dysfunctional. Top performers will disengage.

Be Positive   Undesirable, unpleasant things happen in every organization and in everyone's life. You can make decisions about how you are going to encounter what life brings. Focus on what is good in your situation. Be optimistic about the future. Make a meaningful difference for the people you touch every single day. Engage in your work with enthusiasm. Be someone who improves the morale of your team.

Conduct Yourself with Class   Do things the right way. Be clear about your values. Conduct yourself with impeccable integrity to those values. Lift others up. Do not tear them down. Do not complain. Do not speak about others off

231

the record. Be honest, authentic, and transparent. Ignore gossip. Do not put your self-interest above what is best for the organization.

Make Friends   Many people say, "This is not a popularity contest." Don't be fooled. You will get a lot more done in any community if people genuinely like you. Be nice. Be interested in others. Be a good listener. Be helpful. Be kind. Make as many friends as you can in your organization. And do it with sincerity and pure intent, not with some ulterior motive.

Practice Diplomacy   When disputes occur, listen to understand the other person's perspective, and engage constructively to resolve problems. Seek win-win solutions. Choose your words thoughtfully to make your points without offending the other person or causing him or her to feel criticized. You do not have to say, "That's ridiculous!" You can simply say, "I disagree." Learn how to disagree without being disagreeable.

Confront Bad Behavior   Bad behavior should be confronted, but you can do it diplomatically, as discussed before. You can say, "This is how the situation looks to me. Do you understand how it can be viewed that way?" Usually, you can avoid the word, "wrong." You can say instead, "I think that was an error." Do not demonize people with whom you disagree.

Pick Your Battles   Pick your battles. Some things you just need to let go. Decide thoughtfully when you want to take a stand. You will not win them all. Win or lose, accept the decision and move on. There are times when you will feel good about advocating for your position, even though the decision did not go your way.

Here is a story from Larry about rising above.

Dick Self-Destructs

In 1997, I became the general manager of the Elms Resort and Spa in Excelsior Springs, Missouri. The Elms is a beautiful, charming hotel that first opened in the late 1800s. When I came on board, the hotel was undergoing a complete renovation. It was a construction site. When a hotel is under construction, the construction project manager is in charge. As the construction nears its conclusion, the hotel general manager takes over as the hotel staff prepares to welcome their first guests.

Traditionally, there is tension between the construction project manager and the hotel general manager regarding who gets to make what decisions. I was determined that would not happen at the Elms. I decided that I would be collaborative and deferential in my dealings with the project manager, and that I would not engage in a power struggle over who was in charge.

Despite my sincere efforts, I was unable to develop a positive working relationship with the project manager, whose name was Dick. Dick was actively trying to undermine me. He excluded me from certain important meetings, and he withheld information. He insulted me in public, and at one point he actually withheld my paycheck for two weeks (pleading a temporary cash shortage).

I refused to respond in kind. I continued to treat him with respect and deference, and I continued to invite him to collaborate. I was not a doormat. I picked my battles thoughtfully, and I practiced the seven principles set forth earlier.

My senior executives wanted me to fight with him. I said, "Just wait. He is humiliating himself. As time goes on, people will see who he is, and they will see who I am. It will become evident that Dick is doing great damage to himself and to the organization."

Sure enough, Dick gained zero moral authority and zero legitimacy as a leader. He was unable to deliver on his responsibilities and was fired by the owner of the hotel.

LESSON

It is not wise to ignore the political implications of your decisions and actions. But you do not have to let the politics dictate your actions. You are not in control of what others say and do. You can rise above the politics by focusing on the seven principles stated above. If you do those things and politics still hold you back, start looking for another job right away. You can do better.

EXPERIMENT: RISE ABOVE POLITICS

1. Review the seven principles described earlier, and pick one to improve on.
2. Consciously work on that principle for 90 days.
3. Reflect on how that has affected your situation.
4. Once you are satisfied with your performance of the first principle you chose, pick another and work on that.

Chapter 60

DON'T CHASE HEARSAY, RUMORS, OR GOSSIP

Rumors, hearsay, and gossip damage your culture. Do not condone this kind of communication and do not participate in it.

Have you ever played the telephone game? You get a group of 10 people to form a line. You whisper a message to the first person in line. For example, you could whisper, "Shirley said that Dan has been misrepresenting the data on the study we did for Important Client, Inc." Any message will do. You say it once and only once. The first person then whispers the message to the next person in line and so on to the final person in line. The final person then announces out loud the message they received. In almost every case, the degree of distortion is remarkable.

The game makes a point about third-party information. Rumors, hearsay, and gossip are all examples of third-party information. When someone is giving you third-party information, for example, "Tom said that Kurt . . . ," beware. You did not hear what Tom said. You have no idea whether Tom said anything at all. Regarding Kurt, you have no actionable information. In fact, you can probably think of many times when two people who were in the same meeting gave very different reports about who said what in the meeting. In our example, this third-party information almost certainly tells you more about the person delivering it than it does about either Tom or Kurt.

Many managers are tempted to speak to Tom and/or Kurt to verify the "information" they have received. Resist that temptation. Any action on your part in response to third-party information decreases your productive performance. You are allowing unreliable statements to direct how you use your time and focus your energy. If you act, you are giving your employees positive reinforcement for this behavior, which will bring you similar hearsay in the future. Even worse, when people see you responding this way, they are more likely to do it too, and it becomes a part of your culture. The damage to morale and productivity can be staggering.

LESSON

Hearsay, rumors, and gossip are inevitable. They are impossible to eliminate. You are not going to stop them. But you do not have to reinforce this behavior by taking action based on hearsay. *Do not allow people to control you in this way.*

EXPERIMENT: QUIT REINFORCING HEARSAY, RUMORS, AND GOSSIP

1. The next time someone brings you third-party information, ask the person why they are telling you this and respond accordingly.
2. If the person X has a problem with person Y, tell X to speak to Y, not to you.
3. If this person needs help managing conflict on their own, refer to Chapter 8 for coaching strategies to help them. Other than that . . .
4. Do not act. Do not try to verify what you have heard. Do not do anything. Go about your business. Focus your time and energy on activities that add value and make your organization better.
5. Keep this up for 90 days and reflect on what has changed for you and your team.

SPEAK POSITIVELY ABOUT THOSE NOT PRESENT

G reat managers appropriately place a high value on loyalty. When the chips are down, they want to know that they can rely on the loyalty of their people. But loyalty must flow in both directions.

It is easy to criticize, to find fault, to tear others down—in large and small ways. How often do groups of employees go out after work and complain about the boss, or about other employees? This kind of activity is widespread, but it cannot be characterized as harmless. It hurts people, including those who engage in it. There is a reason people would not want their negative remarks shared with their targets. Do not let this type of behavior become part of your culture.

This type of disloyal behavior is damaging in several ways.

1. It reinforces the speaker's misgivings about the person being discussed.
2. It leaves a negative impression in the mind of the listeners—not only about the person being discussed, *but also about the speaker.*
3. When it gets back to the person being discussed (and it usually does) it reduces engagement and destroys trust.
4. It causes the targets to doubt their actions or decisions, which undermines their ability to perform with excellence.
5. It hurts the positive-negative ratio for everyone involved.

If this type of behavior is part of your culture, what do you think people say about you when you are not present? If you believe you are exempt, you are fooling yourself.

What do you say about your people when they are not present? When you are with a group of your peers and they start telling amusing stories about the deficiencies of their people, do you join in? Or do you say, "My people are terrific!" and tell a story about a recent success? Do you stand up for them? Like many of the suggestions we have offered for shaping your culture, this only works when the positive things you say about people are true. (And what did your mother teach you about what to say when you have nothing nice to say?)

Assuming you are being honest and sincere, what happens when you are 100 percent positive and supportive of your people when they are not present?

1. It reinforces your belief in the person being discussed.
2. It leaves a positive impression in the mind of the listeners.
3. When it gets back to the person being discussed, it builds trust, increases engagement, and intensifies loyalty.
4. It increases your moral authority.
5. It causes your employees who benefit from it to believe in themselves and strive to live up to your expectations. It improves their ability to perform with excellence.
6. You contribute to a healthier, more positive culture.

LESSON

Speak only positively about people who are absent. If you do not have something positive to say, follow the advice your mother gave you and say nothing. This will enhance your moral authority, build trust with your people, and improve your culture.

EXPERIMENT: TALK PEOPLE UP

1. When you are out with associates or in a meeting, do not speak negatively about people who are not present.
2. Find something positive (and true) to say about the person under discussion or don't say anything.
3. Change the topic if necessary.
4. After six months, reflect on what you have learned. Is there less negative talk about others when you are present? Do you think your people have noticed that you support them when they are not present? How has this affected your reputation?

EMBRACE CHANGE

Chapter 62

EMBRACE UNCERTAINTY, BE CONFIDENT, INSTILL HOPE

The pace of change is accelerating. In today's world, managing change is not something you have to do sometimes. You have to do it every day.

The invention and widespread use of antibiotics created superbugs. The invention of the Internet and mobile devices has created privacy and security issues. At the time of this writing, the widespread availability of sophisticated drones is creating a new set of problems. You can likely cite several additional examples.

As you resolve current problems at work, new ones arise. You might anticipate some of these and proactively create strategies to deal with them. But progress is precarious because it always gives birth to unexpected consequences. The immense complexity of the world prevents you from anticipating all the new problems you will face.

So if you are making progress, you are creating new problems, which require new solutions, which create new problems. This is a relentless cycle.

A rational argument for change, a business case, provides justification, but it does not create the energy necessary to move forward. Rational arguments should be put forth, but expecting people to act rationally is folly because our decisions and actions are heavily influenced by emotions, cognitive biases (one of which is the negative bias), and context. Daniel Kahneman summarizes and explains the extensive research that has led to that basic conclusion in his book, *Thinking, Fast and Slow*.[1] Fear is an extremely powerful emotion, and the negative bias is pervasive. Both must be addressed and overcome to make change possible.

Change always involves risks, and fear of the unknown is ever-present. Part of your job as a manager is to encourage your followers. Courage is not the absence of fear. Courage is moving forward despite the presence of fear. To encourage is to motivate people to move forward—to take risks and move into the unknown.

Your self-confidence and genuine caring attracts others. Your passion and determination are contagious. Your belief in the capability of your team is empowering. That is how you manage in ways that help people move forward in spite of the fear.

Our friend, Mark Epp, includes the following phrase in his email signature: "To success and beyond . . ." What is beyond? Hope. Continuous learning and growth, generated by the "new solution, new problem" cycle. Embrace it joyfully. Help your people adopt this mind-set. It will make a big difference in their lives.

LESSON

The truth is that the future is always unknown. Welcome the future, with all its uncertainty. Instill hope by reminding people that this situation presents the real possibility for improvement and growth. Demonstrate optimism and confidence that no matter what happens, you will figure it out together.

We do not purport to provide a comprehensive guide to managing change in this book. The following chapters, however, do provide some specific recommendations about things you can do to improve your ability to manage change.

ENCOURAGE SUGGESTIONS

Have an Appetite for New Ideas

When employees make suggestions, it is a strong indication they are thinking! They are bringing their brains to work. Given the relentless rate of change in the world today, no organization can afford to have employees at any level who merely do what they are told. We all need people who bring their brains to work, and we need to foster cultures that have an appetite for new ideas.

Most of us (probably all of us) care where a new idea comes from. If it comes from someone we see as a respected authority on the topic, we immediately believe the idea is worthy of serious consideration. If it comes from a 21-year-old, brand-new employee we might not give it as much weight. Or, God forbid, it comes from a new hire who just joined us from a competitor. In that case, we might even be very defensive. To what extent should the *where* or the *who* influence how we respond to an idea?

In many organizations, experienced new hires attract criticism when they say, "In my former company we did X, and it worked really well." If that new hire came from a highly successful company, they might discuss their former company frequently, particularly just after they come on board. For some reason, many managers find this annoying. Sometimes, in fact, these new hires are told to stop mentioning their former company.

Why not welcome these statements? When managers make people feel like these statements are unwelcome, they are shutting out opportunities to learn. Do you think that you have nothing to learn from other organizations? These new hires are sharing best practices (or at least practices that are better than the ones they are seeing in your organization). What is the danger? Where is the harm?

Not only should you welcome these ideas, you should give them serious consideration. Reject fear-based responses, and do not immediately dismiss these ideas as, "Not a fit with our culture." Also, be careful about making another common response: "We tried that before. It did not work." Do responses of that sort encourage more suggestions? Do they contribute to learning? The answers are, "No," and "No."

Think of it this way. Suppose you are just walking down the street and find an idea written on a piece of paper. You are with a couple of associates who work with you. There is no way to know who or where this idea came from. Some of you immediately think the idea is worth pursuing, and some of you do not. Your only course of action is to discuss it on its merits. When someone makes a suggestion, that moment is an opportunity for learning, both for the employee and for the manager. *Do Not Waste It!!* Discuss these ideas on their merits. In fact, why not give them a try?

Is your initial reaction to search for flaws? Instead of giving an unsupportive, knee-jerk response, why not give a supportive, knee-jerk response? Here is an example: "Thanks for thinking about ways we can improve. When can we get together to discuss it more? I want to understand more about how you think this will make us better." If you do not have time now, get out your calendar and make an appointment.

All ideas and all strategies have drawbacks and benefits. The process of discussing and evaluating a suggestion will allow those possible consequences to emerge through discovery. This is how learning occurs.

Equally important, the process conveys that you view the person as worthy of your time. By engaging authentically in this evaluation process, no matter what the outcome, you encourage more ideas, not only from that employee, but also from others (because your people are paying close attention).

One final point. Among other things, leaders are people who have ideas for improvement. Could the employee who frequently brings you ideas for improvement be a future leader?

LESSON

When an employee brings you an idea, you are in a learning moment. Do not shoot it down. Make time to discuss the possible consequences, both good and bad. Be open to the possibility that it might be worth a try. If you engage in open-minded discussion, or if you try the idea, somebody will learn something. *It might be you.*

EXPERIMENT: ENCOURAGE IDEAS

1. The next three occasions an employee brings you an idea that you believe will not work, begin by thanking him or her.
2. Take time to discuss the idea, to really understand his or her thinking. Explore the pros and cons.
3. Remember, even if you have tried it before, the circumstances may be different now. Maybe the idea is not exactly the same. Have an open mind.
4. After you have done this three times, reflect on what you have learned. How did the employee feel? Do you think he or she will contribute more ideas? Do you think it was worth your time?

Chapter 64

DON'T STRIVE FOR 100 PERCENT BUY-IN

This chapter discusses five lessons Larry learned when he served as general manager of The Ritz-Carlton, Tysons Corner. The company asked him to lead an experiment to see whether it was possible to run a luxury hotel according to a model known as self-directed work teams. That journey called for fundamental changes in the way they ran the hotel. Based on Larry's experience, what we have to teach on this topic was learned by actually leading change rather than by just studying it.

LESSON

You will not get 100 percent buy-in.

Seeking 100 percent buy-in will waste a great deal of time and effort. Dr. Margaret Mead is credited with the following insight: "Never doubt that a small group of thoughtful, committed citizens can change the world; indeed, it is the only thing that ever has."

EXPERIMENT: WORK WITH THE EARLY ADOPTERS

1. Identify the people who are passionate about the change.
2. Start working with those people immediately on implementing the change.
3. You will notice that over time more employees get on board with what you are doing.
4. Notice that you will achieve significant change without 100 percent buy-in.

LESSON

Fundamental change always involves loss. Allow people to grieve their emotional loss without judgment. If you trivialize the loss, you devalue the person. This does not increase their willingness to support the change or to support you as a manager.

Fundamental change brings about an emotional loss for many who are affected. This loss occurs even though they acknowledge the benefits of the change. For example, if I am a genius at using a slide rule, I can intellectually acknowledge that the organization is better off giving people calculators. But now I am the best at a skill that was highly valued yesterday and is now completely irrelevant. I have experienced a loss.

LESSON

People will have reasonable questions that you cannot answer. Do not be defensive about that. Accept it as part of the change process, and express confidence that you will figure out the answer together.

If you wait until you have all the answers to all the questions, you will never move out to implement the change. Be prepared to figure things out as you go. Articulate that thought as a necessary part of the change process, and work alongside the people you manage to answer their reasonable questions together, as you go along.

LESSON

You will always have a "Back to Egypt" committee.

In preaching about change, a minister once opined that when Moses led the Israelites out of Egypt, and they were struggling with the hardships of wandering in the desert, there was probably a group of followers who advocated returning to Egypt. There will always be a "Back to Egypt" committee—people who actively oppose the change.

Managers often create negative consequences for those people. That approach is counterproductive. Every change involves drawbacks as well as benefits. Every change involves a great deal of ambiguity and numerous questions that cannot be answered at the beginning. This is frightening for some people, even if it is not frightening for you. Punishing people for stating their fears and concerns merely drives their resistance underground, where you, as the manager, cannot participate in the dialogue and help influence the right outcomes.

LESSON

Use your power to move the organization forward, but do so compassionately.

Even though you are encouraging people to publicly express doubts, fears, and concerns, continue to be clear that the train has left the station. You are not reconsidering the change. You can do this compassionately: "I understand that you disagree with this change. I'll do everything in my power to help you make the necessary adjustments. But we're moving forward with this change."

EXPERIMENT: DISCUSS FEARS AND CONCERNS PUBLICLY

1. Encourage public discussion of fears and concerns
2. Do not label people as negative just because they express some fears or concerns
3. Respond to those fears and concerns publicly.
4. Validate concerns and express passionate confidence in your team's ability to find solutions to these issues.
5. Make it clear that you are not reconsidering the change.
6. Pay attention to how these conversations affect your people.

Chapter 65

TAKE ACTION ON LEGACY EMPLOYEES

In times of change, managers have to deal with legacy employees. Many of these people have been loyal, hard-working, and good ambassadors for your company. But your business is changing in ways that are not favorable to some of them. These employees helped you get to where you are now, and you truly appreciate their contributions. It is not their fault, but some of these people are no longer a good fit for the company. What do you do?

This is a common situation. It is difficult for everyone involved. As a manager, you must balance the needs of multiple stakeholders:

1. One employee, or a few, who have been loyal to your organization
2. Other employees who are making the shift more successfully
3. Your organization's clients, customers, guests, or patients
4. The people whose interests you ultimately serve—shareholders, taxpayers, donors, owners, and so forth

All the potential solutions we offer here have painful side effects. What are your alternatives? We suggest you start here:

Allow them to continue in their current role, giving them the opportunity to meet the current expectations for the role.

This is the most attractive option for us, and it is the best place to start. Expectations have evolved with changes in the business and some of your employees are not evolving at the same rate. Clarify the new performance expectations. Give them all the support and help you reasonably can. But hold them accountable. This alternative demonstrates strong loyalty to individuals who are struggling with change, without compromising your duty to other stakeholders or your ability to maximize organizational performance. We recommend you try this alternative first. Then, if they cannot meet the expectations, revert to one of the other options listed here.

Recast them into another job.

This could require them to take a pay cut, or you could decide to grandfather their compensation. Either way, at least they still have a job. This alternative demonstrates a balance between loyalty to these individuals and your duty to maximize benefits to stakeholders.

Terminate their employment, with severance and help.

Unfortunately, recasting is often impossible, either for the organization or for the person. You could give the person a generous severance package, and you could extend yourself to help him or her find another job. This shows some loyalty and empathy for the employee, while emphasizing benefits to stakeholders.

Terminate their employment without severance or help.

We think this is an undesirable way to go. It maximizes benefits to stakeholders, but it demonstrates no loyalty at all. Your employees will get the message. You expect loyalty, but you do not reciprocate. If you choose this option, do not state that loyalty is a core value that defines your culture. This, at least, allows you to avoid hypocrisy.

Carry them. Allow them to continue in their present role, even though they cannot meet the current expectations for the role.

This can be an attractive option at first glance. Perhaps some of these people are close to retirement. You could demonstrate outstanding loyalty by carrying them and simply tolerating their deficiencies. However, this alternative requires extra investment to compensate for these deficiencies, and does not maximize benefits to stakeholders—especially other employees who will likely be doing most of the carrying. This kind of tolerance for poor performance does not enhance your image as a manager. Do not choose this option for people who are not very close to retirement. Even for people who are nearing retirement, the recasting and severance with help options discussed in this chapter are better.

LESSON

Times of change can be particularly difficult for legacy employees. Do not avoid dealing with this head-on. Be thoughtful and compassionate, but take action.

REPLACE EMPLOYEES WHO ARE BLOCKING CHANGE

There are situations in which senior leaders have decided that rapid, major change is required for the survival of the organization. These types of situations are qualitatively different from situations discussed in previous chapters. These are not situations in which change can be accomplished gradually or incrementally. You do not have time for that.

Rapid change requires that certain people leave the organization, either because they willfully resist it or because the change eliminates their jobs. It is unpleasant. It is painful. It is regrettable. But it is reality. This applies to employees at every level. If a particular employee cannot or will not adapt and enthusiastically support this kind of change, he or she must be replaced. To achieve rapid culture change, leaders and managers can't be patient.

If the need for rapid change requires changes in personnel, you, as a manager, will likely be at the tip of the spear. Make those personnel changes with compassion, but do it swiftly. Drawing out the time frame increases the pain and stress for everyone. Also, the turnover you are creating intentionally, cascades through the organization and creates additional, unwanted turnover. The more rapidly you begin with the intentional turnover, the more quickly you will be able to see all of the dominoes that fall as a result and take action to get the right people in place.

These departing employees are, in a sense, casualties of war. You should treat them with respect and dignity, but you need to transition them out of the organization quickly. Then, of course, you need to identify new employees who fit what the organization has become as a result of this rapid change. As a manager, you must be proactive and bring a sense of urgency to helping the new people build positive relationships as quickly as possible, and you must invest significant time in getting to know them individually. (Remember how activities like Focus On You from Chapter 2 and Career Investment Discussions from Chapter 7 can be helpful in that process).

Rapid change is painful and confusing for all stakeholders, and it is very likely to change your organization's culture, whether you want it to or not. Even for people who stay, some things that were highly desirable about working for the organization before may be lost. These kinds of unanticipated consequences are inevitable. For a manager, working through these types of challenges requires a great deal of intestinal fortitude. And if managers lack either the authority or the willingness to replace people, the organization cannot achieve rapid, fundamental change.

LESSON

To bring about rapid change, you must be prepared to replace employees who cannot or will not be a part of the future the organization envisions. Do it compassionately, but do it swiftly. Be proactive in helping new employees build positive relationships quickly.

EXPERIMENT: REPLACE EMPLOYEES WHO BLOCK PROGRESS

1. Identify an employee who is blocking progress on a desired change.
2. Make absolutely sure you have made the expectations and the consequences clear.
3. Make absolutely sure that you have done everything in your power to help this person make the required change.
4. When you reach a day when you are convinced additional efforts will not be successful, let that person go.
5. Invest in selecting the right new employees and optimizing the fit between their talents and the needs and expectations of the organization.
6. Conduct Focus On You sessions to help new employees quickly build positive relationships with other team members.
7. Reflect on what you learned. How did this approach affect your employees? How did it affect your ability to move forward?

Chapter 67

OVERCOMMUNICATE DURING A MANAGEMENT TRANSITION

Management transitions present a unique set of challenges. Consider this situation. The former manager is gone and the successor has yet to be identified. Everyone is confronting the great unknown, and typically the people on the team are not in control of the outcome. It is a scary, stressful time for those people.

Communication is a very important factor in reducing the stress. During the search for the replacement, complete transparency is most often not achievable—partly because candidates do not want to jeopardize their current position. So you cannot announce who is under consideration. Also, the candidate pipeline is in continuous flux, with candidates in different stages of the selection process. The moment you update your team, the readings on the flux capacitor will have changed. Although they will understand this intellectually, it provides little or no emotional comfort. It is still scary. But give them as much information as you can, as frequently as you can.

Listening (the other half of communication) is also monumentally important. Ask people about their concerns. Ask them for their thoughts and suggestions. Ask them how you can best support them during this situation. And most importantly, find things you can do immediately based on what you have heard.

Appoint an acting leader so team members have someone who is carrying their flag, meeting their needs, setting direction, and dealing with outstanding issues. This acting leader should make firm decisions, which will reduce the general air of uncertainty. Also, make sure the former manager's boss invests some time with these individuals, to give them strong support and to demonstrate their significance to the organization.

Do everything you can to keep people focused on productive activities, and highlight successes and progress. But be understanding and tolerant. Different individuals will deal with this stressful situation differently. You might see some behaviors you would rather not see. Negative relationships and other forms of dysfunction could intensify. Teams that go into this situation with strong, positive relationships are better equipped to weather this storm.

One final note. Larry was in this situation once. Here is the story.

The New General Manager

I was a hotel human resources director when the general manager, whom we loved and respected, got transferred. We, the direct reports, were really bummed out. Because we loved this guy so much, we could not imagine a better future. It could only get worse. The transition time was very stressful.

After a while our new boss arrived. Short, German guy. Name of Horst Schulze. Although we could not conceive of it during the transition period, our situation actually improved. Horst was much better than the former general manager. Under his leadership, our business results improved, our service improved, our culture improved, and we all grew as hoteliers and as leaders. By the way, Horst became one of my most significant mentors, and also a good friend.

LESSON

Overcommunicate, and put even more effort into listening. Be tolerant if some people are not their best selves during this stressful time. Consciously remind people that this situation presents the real possibility for improvement and growth. It is quite possible that things will get better.

We know that most readers are not, at this time, in a position to deal with management transitions. But many of you will soon be in more senior positions. We hope you remember the lesson of this chapter at that time.

Chapter 68

PREPARE FOR THE UNKNOWABLE FUTURE

An associate recently asked, "What can managers do to prepare for the future?" We are under no delusion that we have a definitive answer, but it is certainly an important question, well worth discussing (for us) and addressing (for you).

First, we must acknowledge that we can't prepare for all possible future states. That certainly does not mean we should throw up our hands and wait for our fates to unfold. It does mean we should be intentional about deciding which potentialities to prepare for. Paying attention to emerging trends can help us make some decisions. Periodic SWOT analyses (or some similar exercise) can help as well. Many of the most important opportunities and threats, however, are unknowable today because unpredictable events dramatically change the economic and competitive landscape. Here are a few examples: earthquakes, terrorist attacks, the creation of the polio vaccine, the discovery of the Zika virus, the invention of the personal computer (then the laptop, the Blackberry, the smartphone).

LESSON

Many of tomorrow's most important opportunities and threats are unknowable. The future is unpredictable. Something you have never even thought of, something that does not exist right now could change everything in ways you can't even imagine from where you sit.

Focusing on these fundamentals can position you to be prepared for however the future unfolds:

- Select and develop highly talented people.
- Ask those people what they want to learn and give them opportunities to learn it.
- Encourage them to give suggestions and to ask questions.
- Improve your system of listening to your customers to better meet their needs.
- Cultivate a culture of creativity, innovation, and experimentation.
- Be the kind of person who asks, "What if . . ." and bring your questions, ideas, and suggestions to your own leader.

EXPERIMENT: INCREASE YOUR AGILITY BY LISTENING TO YOUR CUSTOMERS

1. Work with your team to create a better system for understanding what your customers want and need.
2. Ask customers these four questions:
   a. What do you really like that we should keep doing?
   b. What should we stop doing (or do less of)?
   c. What should we start doing that we are not doing now?
   d. What should we do better?
3. When you have asked enough customers, choose one or two things to change.
4. Implement the selected changes.
5. After six months, reflect on what you have learned.

In today's world, an appetite for change is a competitive advantage. Be hungry.

INVEST IN YOUR OWN GROWTH

Chapter 69

DEVELOP YOURSELF

No human being ever actualizes his or her full potential outside of the right relationships. Parenting, mentoring, and coaching exemplify the kinds of relationships that can help shape a person and lead to significant growth. So how does self-development fit in?

Each of us matures at our own pace. But whatever the pace, as we mature, we assume more and more responsibility for the outcomes in our lives. Younger or less experienced people often benefit from the mentoring and coaching of people who see their potential and decide to invest in it. By the time you are an adult, you should assume some responsibility for investing in your own potential. Mentors and others can help you with this, but you must be an active participant in the process. For example:

1. A mentor can get you involved with a variety of activities and assignments to help you discover your aptitudes and interests. But you must enthusiastically engage.
2. A mentor can ask what you are passionate about and can help you pursue those passions in ways that contribute to your growth. But your passions must arise from your heart. Your mentor is not responsible for installing them.
3. A mentor can help you ideate about various career arcs, but you must own your goals and your path.
4. A mentor may see something in you and choose to invest. But, as you mature, your responsibility increases for seeing something you can learn from a mentor and initiating that relationship yourself.

Mentors exert a great influence on their mentees. But influence is not ownership. At some point in your journey, you should assume the responsibility for your development. You should articulate a vision for your future. You should be clear about your values and goals. Mentors and others can help, but you have to own it. The final decisions are ultimately yours.

With regard to self-development, what's in it for you? Nothing more or less than taking charge of your future.

Through this journey, you can gain a more profound understanding of your values, commitments, and personal mission in the world. You can gain insights about how to align your strengths, your passions, and your aspirations. After creating your own blueprint, you can ask your mentor or supervisor, "Will you support this plan? How can we improve it? Is there anything else I need to think about?" Then you will be leading your own development.

The following chapters will help you take charge of your own development and thus empower you to continuously increase the difference you are making in the lives of others.

DEFINE WHAT SUCCESS MEANS TO YOU

Defining success is a challenging and nuanced philosophical exercise. The answer is profoundly personal and, therefore, different for each individual. If you devote your life to a cause you deem worthy, but you do not achieve your goals, are you a success? If you achieve your goals, but were dishonest in your approach, are you a success? If your art is not appreciated during your lifetime, are you a success? The answers are up to you and only you.

Moreover, as we gain wisdom, as our perspective evolves, the answer might well change. So we are all well-advised periodically to reflect on this question: What does success mean to me? The struggle to find the answer will likely generate more value than the answer itself.

LESSON

Each person defines success for him- or herself. The struggle to find the answer will likely generate more value than the answer itself.

The answer to the question about success begins with the ancient maxim, "Know thyself."

EXPERIMENT: KNOW THYSELF

Answer the following questions. Some questions are similar, but each is a slightly different stimulus and could evoke a different response. This will take some time, and might involve revision and refinement. In terms of your personal growth, it is well worth the investment.

1. What kind of person do I want to be?
2. What is important to me?
3. In my heart of hearts, what do I value most?
4. What do I want to accomplish?
5. What do I stand for?
6. What example do I want to set?
7. What values do I want to embody?
8. What are my gifts and strengths?
9. What positive difference do I want to make in the world?
10. What do I want people to say about me at my funeral?
11. Regarding the time I invest in various activities, what is the ideal balance for me?
12. What do I want my legacy to be?

We are always in the process of becoming. Are you doing what you wish to be doing? Are you becoming the person you wish to become? Are you making a difference? If so, we would say you are on the path that is right for you. In our book, that is success.

Chapter 71

SPEND MORE TIME ON THE 20

The law of the vital few, known more formally as the Pareto Principle, helps people focus on the things that make the biggest difference. It is also known as the 80/20 rule. Here are some examples of this rule:

1. Eighty percent of your revenue comes from 20 percent of your customers.
2. Eighty percent of your sales come from 20 percent of your products.
3. Eighty percent of your sales are made by 20 percent of your sales staff.
4. Eighty percent of your employee turnover comes from 20 percent of your departments.

These are always approximations, of course, but the important point is the principle generally holds true.

LESSON

Twenty percent of your efforts account for 80 percent of your results. Time management is not about doing many things at once. It is about spending your time on the things that make the biggest difference.

Here is an example from Larry's experience:

Reducing Accidents

A hotel in which I was working had too many accidents. We had a safety committee that was implementing all the normal strategies, and modest improvements were achieved. The hotel controller, who was not on the committee, reviewed the available data and arrived at the following insight: 80 percent of the accidents occurred around 3 PM, which was the shift-change time. We thereafter focused our efforts on reducing accidents only during that window of time and achieved a dramatic reduction in accidents.

Here is one more example:

A Simple Method to Increase Your Sales

A member of the board of directors of the world-famous Thunderbird School of Global Management shared with me that very early in his career he sold books door to door and he came to the following insight: No matter one's level of sales talent, the more doors one knocked on, the more books one sold. Knocking on doors was the 20.

You will achieve more impressive results faster if you focus your efforts—and the efforts of your team members—on the 20. However, to do that, you must first be clear about your goals and the results you are trying to achieve—your definition of success. Only then can you identify the vital few activities that will contribute the most to your results.

Different goals will produce different answers to the question, "What is the 20?" Often, like knocking on more doors, it is not that complicated. But you must first establish clear goals.

Then, you must relentlessly ask the next question, "Are we working on the 20?" You cannot spend all your time on the 20. But it is so easy to get out of focus and wind up spending time on the easy and the apparently urgent rather than on the vital few activities that make the biggest difference. You wind up working really hard, but on the wrong things.

Nobody can get everything done these days. Working on the 20 ensures that the things you spend time on are more important than the things you do not work on.

EXPERIMENT: SPEND MORE TIME ON THE 20

1. Clarify your goals.
2. In light of those goals, answer the question, "What are the one or two vital activities that will make the biggest difference in achieving those goals?"
3. Note: some of those activities might be important, but not urgent.
4. Schedule time to work on the 20.
5. After 90 days, reflect on what you have learned. How successful were you in spending more time on the 20? If you successfully increased your time on those vital few activities, what happened as a result?

Chapter 72

BUILD YOUR STRENGTHS

Building your strengths is entirely consistent with focusing more on the 20. We discussed earlier in this book the importance of developing your people by investing in their areas of strength rather than remediating weaknesses. As we have said, there is a difference between room for improvement and potential for improvement. The same principles apply to you.

Working on areas of weakness yields minimal improvement after great effort. It undermines self-esteem. Working on areas of giftedness yields rapid improvement, upbeat engagement, and enhanced self-esteem if the area of giftedness is something a person enjoys doing. That "if" is critical. There are certainly some things you can do better than anyone else, but you do not enjoy doing them. No matter how talented you may be, trying to grow in an area you do not enjoy will feel like pushing a rope uphill.

The best managers and executives are self-aware and align their work accordingly. It is a sign of intelligence and self-confidence to acknowledge what you are good at and not good at, and what you like and do not like to do. The best managers and executives also surround themselves with people who possess strengths that are complementary to their own. They take full advantage of what other people are good at and enjoy in order to help those people grow and to achieve the highest levels of performance.

LESSON

Your strengths are things you are naturally good at *and* enjoy. Your biggest potential for growth lies in developing your gifts and areas of strength.

The more time you spend in your areas of strength, the more value you will create for your organization, and the faster you will grow. Using your gifts is inherently enjoyable most of the time, but pay attention to when it is not, and spend less time in activities that are less enjoyable, even if they are relative areas of strength. When you invest in developing your strengths with an eye on what you enjoy (and when you do that for others), you will improve engagement, retention, and productive performance while reducing stress and improving well-being.

EXPERIMENT: BUILD YOUR STRENGTHS

1. Make a list of the things you are good at and like to do.
2. Pick at least one of your strengths and find a way to develop it. Ask your supervisor to help you spend more time using that strength. Take a course. Attend a seminar. Hang out with others who share that strength. There are numerous ways to grow in that area.
3. After six months reflect on how you have grown and what that growth has done for you and your organization.

IF YOU HAVE BEEN NEWLY PROMOTED, JUST TAKE CHARGE

So you have been promoted to a new role as a manager. On the one hand, this promotion is the culmination of your professional growth to date. On the other hand, it marks the beginning of an entirely new cycle of growth for you, one in which you will need to be an even more active participant. If your promotion involves taking responsibility for managing people who were previously your peers (within the same team or organization), you will face unique challenges. The suggestions that follow can help you maximize your success.

Act with Confidence   Give direction in a matter-of-fact way. Make it clear through your conversational tone of voice and your relaxed demeanor that you expect people to follow your direction. Do not act like you have something to prove (you have already proven it). Do not take an apologetic approach either. As our friend and client Jim Beglin says, "When in charge, take charge." Do not be afraid to rock the boat by changing things. If you are a good manager, you will want to improve things, which requires change. Taking that kind of responsibility seriously is part of investing in your own development as a manager.

Hold People Accountable   Do not try to maintain your status as "one of the team." You have been promoted. Your relationship with the members of your team has changed. You can still be friends—we encourage it! (See Chapter 3.) But do not allow your former peers to take unfair advantage of your friendship. Clarify that you intend to be their ally, not their judge, and hold each person accountable. Your people need you to hold them accountable because it will spur their growth and the growth of the team. And you must do it for your own growth and success as a manager, as well.

Keep an Open Door and an Open Mind Remember the advice of Stephen R. Covey:[1] *You can be effective with people, but you can't be efficient.* Give each person the time they need, ideally when they need it. Doing so demonstrates powerfully that they are significant to you.

Show your team members that you respect and honor their knowledge, experience, and capabilities. Demonstrate this respect by asking people for their opinions and for their help on specific projects or tasks. Make it clear that you are thankful to have them on the team.

When you encounter undesired attitudes and behaviors, first seek to understand the *why. Your assumption that you know the* why *without asking is usually mistaken.*

Help People Grow As a manager, you are responsible for helping other people do their best work. When you help them grow, you are investing in your own growth because each time you help someone else improve or grow, you have achieved the essential work that defines highly effective management.

Conduct a Career Investment Discussion (see Chapter 7) with each direct report within the first month. Find something you can do on each person's behalf that will help him or her grow.

Work actively to help people succeed and to realize their aspirations. As our colleague Jim Meehan[2] advises, enliven the following principle: "I mean you no harm; I seek your greatest good." Put the well-being of your people ahead of your own self-interest, realizing that what you do for them comes back to you.

LESSON

Managing former peers presents unique challenges. A good manager makes things better. If you manage with excellence, over time even the doubters will recognize (sometimes begrudgingly) that they are better off, and they will support you in your new role.

EXPERIMENT: JUST TAKE CHARGE

1. Act in accordance with the points set out in this chapter.
2. After 90 days, review what you have learned. Is your former status as a peer even an issue anymore?

IF YOU FEEL TRAPPED IN YOUR JOB, CHANGE SOMETHING

Part of developing yourself involves taking ownership for how you feel about your work. Too many people hate their jobs. For them, almost every day is a bad day. Aside from the negative impact this has on performance and engagement, it increases stress and anxiety, which has a negative impact on physical, mental, and emotional health. In many cases, people who hate their jobs bring that stress and negativity into their homes, which hurts their family and their friends. If you hate your job, if you are frequently experiencing bad days, if you feel trapped in your job, this chapter is for you.

Organizations and managers should be intentional and aggressive about creating a culture in which people feel valued, significant, and fulfilled, a culture in which people truly look forward to going to work. It is also the case, however, that each of us must take responsibility for the outcomes in our lives. Your life decisions have put you in your current situation. You might feel trapped, but you are not trapped.

Your first option is to change something external. Change some aspect of your current job or start looking for another job where you will look forward to going to work, a job in which you have no problem saying that what you are getting out of it is worth the cost. Changing jobs, however, involves great risk and often great cost. You might not be ready for a life decision like this. You might decide that, at this time, it is best for you to stay in a job you do not like. That is a completely rational choice, but in that case, change your thinking. You are not really trapped if you make a conscious decision to stay in the situation. Embrace the situation and remind yourself that you have decided to pay this cost in order to receive the benefits and outcomes you seek. Stress is caused by resistance to what is. We know this is not easy, but you can make a commitment to work on it.

Here is a brief account of Larry's personal experience with this situation:

The Career Change

I used to practice law. I made good money but I was not fulfilled. After a long period of introspection, I decided to make a career change, which required a substantial pay cut. I decided to pay that cost. I got into a career I loved, and I have never had a moment's regret about that decision.

Subsequent to that, I had a job in which I traveled more than 200 days a year on business. I hated the travel, but I loved what I got to do when I arrived at my destination. I had to constantly remind myself that the unpleasantness of the travel was part of the cost for me to do what I loved. I never regretted staying in that job.

LESSON

If you are feeling trapped in your job, change something. Change some aspects of your current job or look for another job. If you are unable to change something external, change something internal. Change your thinking. You are not trapped if you consciously embrace your situation.

EXPERIMENT: COST/BENEFIT ANALYSIS

1. If you feel trapped, answer the following questions:
   a. Why do I stay in this job?
   b. What is this costing me? What is it costing my family?
   c. Is what I get from this job worth the cost?
2. If the answer to "c" is yes, change your thinking. Embrace your situation. Remind yourself that your life decisions have brought you to this point. Establish a goal to figure out how to be happy in this situation.
3. If the answer to "c" is no, take action to change something external. Change your job responsibilities or look for another job.

Sometimes everyone needs to blow off some steam. But there is a point at which occasionally blowing off steam morphs into constant complaining and abiding dissatisfaction. Reliving unpleasant experiences evokes more negative feelings and creates additional stress. Recounting your bad day just poisons your evening, not only for you, but also for those around you. When your bad day is over, do not take it with you. Raise your awareness of the present. Notice that in the present moment, nothing bad is happening to you. Do not allow events of the recent past to ruin the present moment. We are aware that this is not easy. But with practice, you can do this more frequently and achieve more happiness in your life as a result.

LESSON

If you cannot leave, and things around you will not change, quit complaining about them. Reliving unpleasant experiences just magnifies negative emotions and poisons your time away from work. Notice that in the present moment nothing bad is happening to you. Do not allow events of the recent past to ruin your ability to enjoy the present moment.

EXPERIMENT: QUIT RELIVING UNPLEASANT EXPERIENCES

1. If you have had a bad day, when someone asks you, "How was your day?" *Do not answer the question!*
2. Raise your awareness. Be present. In the present moment (after your work day), nothing bad is happening to you. Don't let the day's events poison your evening.
3. When someone asks, "How was your day?" say this: "I'd rather not relive those events. I'd rather focus on having a great evening with you."
4. Have a great evening.
5. After 90 days, reflect on what you've learned. How has this changed your relationships with your friends and family? How has this affected your stress level?

In any situation, you can find ways to do more positive and meaningful things at work. Be kind, forgiving, and helpful to your associates. Celebrate their successes, and support them during difficult times. Express appreciation. Be a role model for character. You can make a difference. You can make your organization a better place. To acquaint yourself with a shining example of how to make a positive difference in a truly horrible situation, we recommend Viktor Frankl's book, *Man's Search for Meaning.*[1]

TAKE STEPS TO FIT IN ON A NEW JOB

LESSON

Whether you are a recent graduate accepting your first career position or a seasoned professional making a move after 20 years with the same company, beginning a new job in a new organization presents an important opportunity to grow. To make the most of this opportunity, you should take ownership for discovering what defines the organization culture and doing your best to fit in.

The window of opportunity is never greater than when you are starting a new job. Fitting in allows you to take full advantage of this immense opportunity to accelerate your own growth and development. The following principles will take you a long way toward success.

Dress Appropriately You have visited your new organization at least once, and probably several times before your first day of work. Dress style is a cultural norm, whether or not a formal dress code exists. It is the first thing people see, and it affects their impression. Adjust your style of dress to fit in.

Demonstrate a Consistent, Positive Attitude This appears to be a platitude, but it is not. Your positive attitude is one of the first things people notice about you. And because positivity is contagious, you will add something of value right away.

Work Hard   This is another apparent platitude. But once again, it is immensely important. Everyone appreciates hard work *and* it is very visible. It increases the amount of value you add. If you work hard and you have a positive attitude, you will *immediately* earn a positive reputation in your new organization.

Be Brutally Open-Minded (Thanks to Our Colleague Brent Proulx for This Wonderful Phrase)   A new job is an opportunity for tremendous learning and growth. Be humble. Allow your biases and beliefs to be challenged. Let some time pass before saying, "This is how we did it at my former organization." As Stephen R. Covey[1] taught: First seek to understand, then strive to be understood. If you are sincerely receptive to learning from your new associates, they will be more receptive to learning from you.

Cultivate Positive Relationships   Unless you cultivate positive relationships, you will not fit in rapidly, and you might not ever fit in at all. Over time, cultivating positive relationships is the most important thing you can do.

Make Your Boss's Priorities Your Own   Larry is indebted to one of his mentors, Sigi Brauer, for this insight. This is about adding value. Value, like beauty, is in the eye of the beholder. Demonstrate a sense of urgency in moving forward those things that are important to your boss. Again, it is extremely noticeable, and your boss will sincerely appreciate it.

EXPERIMENT: RATE YOUR EFFORTS TO FIT IN

1. Review the six preceding principles daily for your first 90 days in a new role.
2. Once a week, rate yourself on each of these six principles, using a 1 to 10 scale in which 1 = very poor and 10 = nearly perfect.
3. After 30 days, review how well you are fitting in to the new organization.
4. After 90 days, do another review, and answer the following question, "What advice would you give to a new employee about how to fit in rapidly in this organization?"

HIRE SOME PEOPLE WHO CAN REPLACE YOU

Your investments in your own development are likely to accelerate your career growth. It is easiest to move on in your career when you have someone on your team who can smoothly transition into your role. So when you are selecting people to join your team, make sure you select some people who have the potential to be promoted.

Not every candidate will meet this standard, and not every person on your team needs to be promotable. When you hold to this standard for a new hire, it is likely to take longer to fill that position, but if you hold out for at least some promotable individuals, you will be taking care of your team's future needs.

A consequence of this approach is that you might wind up with more promotion-ready people than you have opportunities. You invest in their development, and then they leave for promotions available in other organizations. That is a great problem to have. You should consider those kinds of moves to be graduations. This is something you should be proud of and something you should publicize. You will earn the reputation of investing in people and preparing them to move forward in their careers. That kind of reputation makes it easier to attract more high-potential people to your organization.

LESSON

There is nothing wrong with selecting someone who can perform the present job with excellence, even though he or she does not have the desire or the potential to be promoted. But if every employee is in this category,

(continued)

> (*continued*)
>
> you will not be able to develop a successor, which could impede your career. You have to hire and invest in developing at least a few employees who have management potential.

It is challenging enough to hold out for top performers who have the potential to perform with excellence in the current open job. There is a sense in which that is not "settling," but it is only hiring for today. Managing to make a difference means that, at least some of the time, you are looking beyond today's needs and hiring for tomorrow.

EXPERIMENT: HOW MANY POTENTIAL FUTURE MANAGERS DO YOU HAVE?

1. How many people on your current team have the potential to take over from you when you are ready to move on in your career?
2. If the number is zero, start looking for candidates who appear to have the potential to be promoted.

Suppose a mid-level manager leaves. Even if you have a deep talent bench, you must still address the question, "Should we select a candidate who can do this role with excellence, or should we select one who also has the potential to be promoted?" Both types of candidates can meet the definition of "high potential." Do you hire for today or tomorrow? We believe it's good to have a balance of both.

FIND A MENTOR

A mentor is someone who takes a special interest in you, who believes in you, who likes you as a person, who enjoys spending time with you, who enjoys helping you grow (both personally and professionally), who is loyal, and who will extend him- or herself to help you succeed. A mentor can play a significant role in your ongoing development. If you are fortunate you will have several mentors over the course of your career.

So, how do you find a mentor? We wish we had an easy answer, or frankly, any answer that would work consistently. The process of finding a mentor is no different from finding a close friend or a life partner. It involves some luck, but there are things you can do to improve the likelihood of success:

Know Yourself It is much easier to find something if you know what you are looking for. Begin by knowing who *you* are, what *you* want to achieve and how *you* define success. Then you can think about what you want to get out of a mentoring relationship and what kind of person your ideal mentor would be.

Look at Your Current Relationships Think about how you formed relationships with other important people in your life. How did you meet your close friends? Your significant other? What were you doing at the time? What were your initial attractions? Why did you both decide you wanted to spend more time with each other? Answering those questions might well provide some valuable insight about how to meet a mentor.

Create Opportunities Participate in professional associations in which you increase the odds of meeting people who share your professional interests and who might be willing to share their knowledge, experience, and wisdom. Community service groups also provide worthwhile opportunities to meet potential mentors.

Make the First Move   Understand that your mentor might not make the first move. You might have to ask the person on the equivalent of a first date. Finding a mentor is really very much like dating. If you do not ask, the possibility will pass you by.

Take It Slow   If you have (or have had) a significant other, think about how you started that relationship. You probably did not jump into a discussion about a long-term relationship right away. You probably just decided whether you wanted to see each other again. If you meet someone you think might be mentor material, do not immediately discuss a mentoring relationship. Just ask him or her out. Have a cup of coffee, lunch, or a glass of wine after work. Get to know each other. See where it goes. Maybe a mentoring relationship will develop over time.

LESSON

Finding a mentor is like developing a close friendship. You should know what kind of a relationship you seek, and you should have an idea about what the right mentor looks like for you. Participate in professional and community organizations to increase your odds of meeting the right person. Know that you might have to make the first move to initiate the relationship.

EXPERIMENT: MAKE THE FIRST MOVE

1. Write down what you want to get out of a mentoring relationship.
2. Write down a description of your ideal mentor.
3. Join one professional and one community organization.
4. When you meet someone who might be that person, ask if he or she would be willing to spend a little time with you. Explain why you are asking.
5. Determine whether you both would like to see each other again. If yes, see where it goes.
6. Repeat steps 4 and 5. Even if you do not find the right mentor at first, you will meet some interesting people and get some good networking done.

In the next chapter, we give some advice about how to be a good mentee.

BECOME A BETTER MENTEE

Although our discussion focuses on the mentoring relationship, the advice in this chapter applies more broadly to any sort of relationship in which you are being coached, advised, or taught by an individual outside a classroom on an ongoing basis.

To begin, we must recognize that this is similar to asking, "How can I become a better spouse?" or "How can I become a better friend?" It is individualized. It depends on the unique needs of each person in the relationship. All this is much easier if the two of you are a good, natural fit in the first place. When the fit is good, you will have to make fewer changes to become a better mentee for that mentor.

Clarify Expectations   Ask your mentor what he or she wants from you in this relationship. This might seem more formal than necessary, but you will both be well served. Too often, in all sorts of relationships, expectations are not clarified, which leads to problems. If your mentor has important expectations that you cannot or do not want to fulfill, it is best to find out as soon as possible.

Larry had a close friend who was a high-powered attorney, dedicated to her career. When she married, she did not know that her husband expected her to cook dinner for him every night, and to otherwise do all the things a non-working spouse would have done in the 1950s. Tragically, it was a deal breaker for both of them.

Take Your Mentor's Advice   As Larry's wife, Salli, says, "Why buy a dog and then bark yourself?" Sometimes, the advice will not intuitively seem like a good idea. When you have misgivings, discuss them. But *take the advice anyway*. Try it despite your doubts. A good mentor will occasionally push you out of your comfort zone. If you reject your mentor's advice too frequently, you should look for another mentor.

Do Not Take Everyone's Advice   Many well-meaning people will offer you advice. Do not treat their advice the same way you treat the advice of your mentor. The relationship is not the same. Suppose you hire a wellness coach. After learning about your goals and challenges, this coach will recommend a program for you to follow. When you share your program with your friends, you will be bombarded with diverging and conflicting advice about the elements of your program. If you act on all this advice, you will not be following a program whose elements have either internal consistency or harmony. You will not make progress. And you will not be honoring the relationship with your wellness coach.

The same principle applies to your mentor and his or her advice. Acting on advice from too many different sources can easily prevent you from progressing. This is not to discourage you from seeking different opinions, just as you might for a medical problem. But before you act, discuss these opinions with your mentor. That way, your decisions and actions will maintain both internal harmony and consistency and you will be communicating in a way that strengthens the bond between you and your mentor.

Honor the Value of Your Mentor's Time   Prepare for your meetings. Come to every meeting with a brief list of problems, challenges, issues, or topics on which you would like input. Listen actively and take notes.

Express Appreciation   Appreciation from a mentee is among the most meaningful forms of recognition a mentor receives. Find ways to express appreciation that are uniquely tailored to your mentor, to the work you have done together, and to the relationship you have cultivated.

LESSON

To become a better mentee, clarify your mentor's expectations of you in the relationship. Take your mentor's advice even when you are not entirely sure it will work. Do not act on advice from others when it conflicts with your mentor's advice. Honor the value of your mentor's time by preparing for meetings. Express appreciation.

EXPERIMENT: BECOME A BETTER MENTEE

1. Rate yourself on each of the principles discussed in this chapter. Use a 1 to 10 scale in which 1 = Very poor and 10 = Nearly perfect.
2. Choose one or two items to work on.
3. After 90 days, assess your effectiveness as a mentee. What have you learned? How has your relationship changed?

EXPRESS YOUR GRATITUDE

We wrote *Managing to Make a Difference* to help you discover strategies, tactics, and techniques that empower you to make a difference in the lives of your employees. Many of these approaches can be used with your friends and family to make a bigger difference in their lives.

In this final chapter, we bring the endeavor of making a difference full circle. We encourage you to reflect on and express gratitude to the people who have made a significant, positive difference in your life.

EXPERIMENT: THANK THOSE WHO MADE A DIFFERENCE IN YOUR LIFE

1. Think about the people whose influence helped you become who you are today, people who have made a significant, positive, and lasting difference in your life.
2. Take a few moments and make a list of their names. No matter your age, the list is not long. Just take a few moments and write their names.
3. Chances are you have not thought about some of these people in a while. Some might have passed away.
4. Visualize each person, one by one.
5. Think about what each one did that influenced you in such a powerful, lasting way.
6. Now, answer this question: Do they know what a huge difference they made in your life? We submit that unless you have told them, they do not know.

(continued)

(continued)

7. Here comes the immensely rewarding part: *tell them.* Tell them in person, or tell them in a handwritten letter. Tell them openly, sincerely, and authentically from your heart.

8. If you are visualizing actually doing this, you might be uncomfortable or even apprehensive. This is normal. This sort of profoundly personal, emotional disclosure is rare in our society. Do it anyway. Do it before you lose the opportunity.

9. Reflect on what you have learned by doing this. How did it make you feel? How did it make them feel? What will you do differently to make a significant, positive, and lasting difference in the lives of the people you care about?

A young man who did this experiment wrote a letter to Larry saying that other than his baptism, it was the most important experience of his life.

Expressing your sincere gratitude to these individuals will be immensely rewarding. For each person you tell, it will be the most meaningful gift that person has received in a very long time.

NOTES

CHAPTER 1

1. John E. Hunter, Frank L. Schmidt, and Michael K. Judiesch, "Individual Differences in Output Variability as a Function of Job Complexity," *Journal of Applied Psychology* 75, no. 1 (February 1990): 28–42. doi:10.1037// 0021–9010.75.1.28.
2. Jennifer Robison, "Turning Around Employee Turnover," *Gallup Business Journal*, May 8, 2008, www.gallup.com/businessjournal/106912/Turning-Around-Your-Turnover-Problem.aspx.
3. Kimberly Schaufenbuel, "Powering Your Bottom Line through Employee Engagement," 2013, www.kenan-flagler.unc.edu/~/media/Files/documents/executive-development/powering-your-bottom-line.pdf.

CHAPTER 6

1. A. K. Przybylski and N. Weinstein, "Can You Connect with Me Now? How the Presence of Mobile Communication Technology Influences Face-to-Face Conversation Quality," *Journal of Social and Personal Relationships* 30, no. 3 (2012): 237–246. doi:10.1177/0265407512453827.

CHAPTER 7

1. Drea Zigarmi, Jim Diehl, Dobie Houson, and David Witt, "Are Employees' Needs Being Met by One-on-Ones? Survey Says 'No,'" *The Ken Blanchard Companies*, 2013, www.kenblanchard.com/getattachment/Leading-Research/Research/Employee-Passion-Volume-6/Blanchard-Employee-Passion-Vol-6 .pdf.

CHAPTER 8

1. Drea Zigarmi, Jim Diehl, Dobie Houson, and David Witt, "Are Employees' Needs Being Met by One-on-Ones? Survey Says 'No,'" *The Ken Blanchard Companies*, 2013, www.kenblanchard.com/getattachment/

Leading-Research/Research/Employee-Passion-Volume-6/Blanchard-Employee-Passion-Vol-6.pdf.

CHAPTER 9

1. Roy J. Lewicki, Beth Polin, and Robert B. Lount, "An Exploration of the Structure of Effective Apologies," *Negotiation and Conflict Management Research* 9, no. 2 (2016): 177–196. doi:10.1111/ncmr.12073.

CHAPTER 10

1. Frederic Luskin, "What Is Forgiveness?" *Greater Good*, August 19, 2010, http://greatergood.berkeley.edu/article/item/what_is_forgiveness.
2. Everett L. Worthington, Jr., "The New Science of Forgiveness," *Greater Good*, September 1, 2004, http://greatergood.berkeley.edu/article/item/the_new_science_of_forgiveness.
3. C. V. O. Witvliet, T. E. Ludwig, and K. L. V. Laan, "Granting Forgiveness or Harboring Grudges: Implications for Emotion, Physiology, and Health," *Psychological Science* 12, no. 2 (2001): 117–123. doi:10.1111/1467-9280.00320.
4. Frederic Luskin, Rick Aberman, and Arthur E. DeLorenzo, Sr., "Effect of Training of Emotional Competence in Financial Services Advisors." Retrieved November 1, 2016, from http://learningtoforgive.com/research/effect-of-training-of-emotional-competence-in-financial-services-advisors.
5. Brooke Deterline, "The Power of Forgiveness at Work," *Greater Good*, August 26, 2016, http://greatergood.berkeley.edu/article/item/the_power_of_forgiveness_at_work.

CHAPTER 17

1. Robert Rosenthal and Lenore Jacobson, "Teachers' Expectancies: Determinants of Pupils' IQ Gains," *Psychological Reports* 19, no. 1 (1966): 115–118. doi:10.2466/pr0.1966.19.1.115.
2. J. Stanley Livingston, "Pygmalion in Management," *Harvard Business Review*, January 2013, https://hbr.org/2003/01/pygmalion-in-management.
3. Annie Murphy Paul, "The Pygmalion Effect: Using Expectations to Generate Success," *The Brilliant Blog*, March 25, 2013, http://anniemurphypaul.com/2013/03/the-pygmalion-effect-using-expectations-to-generate-success.

CHAPTER 21

1. Catherine Bailey, and Adrian Madden, "What Makes Work Meaningful—Or Meaningless," *MIT Sloan Management Review*, June 1, 2016, http://sloanreview.mit.edu/article/what-makes-work-meaningful-or-meaningless.

CHAPTER 46

1. Talya N. Bauer, "Onboarding New Employees: Maximizing Success," *SHRM Foundation's Effective Practice Guideline Series*, 2011, https://www.shrm.org/about/foundation/products/documents/onboarding%20epg-%20final.pdf.

CHAPTER 50

1. Ed Batista, "Building a Feedback-Rich Culture," *Harvard Business Review*, December 24, 2013, https://hbr.org/2013/12/building-a-feedback-rich-culture.

CHAPTER 51

1. Paul Rozin and Edward B. Royzman, "Negative Bias, Negative Dominance, and Contagion." *Personality and Social Psychology Review* 5, no. 4 (2001): 296–320.
2. Roy F. Baumeister, Ellen Bratslavsky, Catrin Finkenauer, and Kathleen D. Vohs, "Bad Is Stronger than Good," *Review of General Psychology* 5, no. 4 (2001): 323–370. doi:10.1037//1089-2680.5.4.323.
3. Michael McIntosh, "Caught in the Act! . . . of Doing Something Right: A Neurobiological Approach to High Performance Management," *21 Triangles*, April 5, 2016, https://www.21triangles.com/Blog/caught-in-the-act-of-doing-something-right-a-neurobiological-approach-to-high-performance-management.
4. Barbara L. Fredrickson, "Updated Thinking on Positivity Ratios," *American Psychologist* 68, no. 9 (2013): 814–822. doi:10.1037/a0033584.
5. Marcial Losada and Emily Heaphy, "The Role of Positivity and Connectivity in the Performance of Business Teams: A Nonlinear Dynamics Model," *American Behavioral Scientist* 47, no. 6 (2004): 740–765. doi:10.1177/0002764203260208.
6. John Mordechai Gottman, *What Predicts Divorce? The Relationship between Marital Processes and Marital Outcomes*. Hillsdale, NJ: Lawrence Erlbaum Associates, 1994.
7. Janice Kaplan, "Gratitude Survey" (Berkeley, CA: John Templeton Foundation, June–October 2012).
8. Adam M. Grant and Francesca Gino, "A Little Thanks Goes a Long Way: Explaining Why Gratitude Expressions Motivate Prosocial Behavior," *Journal of Personality and Social Psychology* 98, no. 6 (2010): 946–955. doi:10.1037/a0017935.
9. Josh Bersin, "New Research Unlocks the Secret of Employee Recognition," *Forbes*, June 13, 2012. www.forbes.com/sites/joshbersin/2012/06/13/new-research-unlocks-the-secret-of-employee-recognition/3.

CHAPTER 55

1. M. J. Tews, J. W. Michel, and A. Bartlett, "The Fundamental Role of Workplace Fun in Applicant Attraction," *Journal of Leadership & Organizational Studies* 19, no. 1 (2012): 105–114. doi:10.1177/1548051811431828.
2. M. J. Tews, J. W. Michel, and K. Stafford, "Does Fun Pay? The Impact of Workplace Fun on Employee Turnover and Performance," *Cornell Hospitality Quarterly* 54, no. 4 (2013): 370–382. doi:10.1177/1938965513505355.

CHAPTER 58

1. Luigi Guiso, Paola Sapienza, and Luigi Zingales, "The Value of Corporate Culture," *Journal of Financial Economics* 117, no. 1 (May 2014): 60–76. doi:10.1016/j.jfineco.2014.05.010.

CHAPTER 62

1. Daniel Kahneman, *Thinking, Fast and Slow* (New York: Farrar, Straus and Giroux, 2011).

CHAPTER 73

1. Stephen R. Covey, *The 7 Habits of Highly Effective People: Restoring the Character Ethic* (New York: Free Press, 2004).
2. Jim Meehan, *I Mean You No Harm; I Seek Your Greatest Good: Reflections on Trust* (iUniverse, 2015).

CHAPTER 74

1. Viktor E. Frankl, *Man's Search for Meaning* (New York: Washington Square Press/Pocket Books, 1985).

CHAPTER 75

1. Stephen R. Covey, *The 7 Habits of Highly Effective People: Restoring the Character Ethic* (New York: Free Press, 2004).

ABOUT THE AUTHORS

Larry Sternberg, JD, Talent Plus Fellow

 Having been with Talent Plus® since 1999, Sternberg has served in a variety of capacities, beginning as a management consultant and in-depth analyst. He has held leadership positions as chair of management consulting, leadership consulting and client engagement, and most recently as president. He is now a member of Talent Plus's board of directors, and a Talent Plus Fellow, performing duties as an often-requested speaker and consultant. His ideation is expressed as an active blogger by writing weekly for the Leadership Laboratory (www.leadershiplaboratory.wordpress.com | www.talentplus.com/talent-plus-viewpoint-blog).

Sternberg has been instrumental in helping clients build Talent-Based Organizations. He has designed and conducted training programs on a variety of topics for thousands of executives and managers and has served as a facilitator for numerous organizations to articulate their mission, vision, and values. His areas of expertise include selection, training and development, employee engagement, empowerment, self-directed work teams, strengths management, mentoring, and leading change. Sternberg's teaching ability and sense of humor have earned him a reputation as one of the most talented and effective teachers and facilitators in the country.

Before joining Talent Plus, Sternberg used the Science of Talent as vice president of human resources with The Portman Hotel Company and as a general manager with The Ritz-Carlton Hotel Company. He pioneered self-directed work teams, achieving remarkable improvements in financial results, guest satisfaction, and employee satisfaction. His approach was described in the book *Turned On: Eight Vital Insights to Energize Your People, Customers, and Profits*, by Roger Dow and Susan Cook.

A native of upstate New York, Sternberg and his wife, Salli, have called Lincoln, Nebraska, their home since 2006. Sternberg holds a BA degree in philosophy from Hamilton College, where he was a member of Phi Beta Kappa, and a Juris Doctor degree from Georgetown University Law Center.

Kim Turnage, PhD

 Kim Turnage has spent her career figuring out where people naturally excel and connecting them with opportunities to stretch those talents. She first joined Talent Plus® in 1997 as a senior research analyst and leadership consultant. At that time, she directed research, statistical analysis, and reporting of results, including the design, initial validation, and ongoing validation of selection instruments. She also consulted with clients to develop and implement measurement strategies to help them understand the impact of talent-based selection and strengths-based management on their business outcomes.

She now serves as a senior leadership consultant at Talent Plus. In this capacity, she works with client partners in the selection, development, and retention of top leadership talent, including succession planning. She has consulted with global clients, including The Ritz-Carlton Hotel Company, Sun International, Cancer Treatment Centers of America (CTCA), Harman Management Corporation, the United States Air Force, and Gensler. She is also a regular contributor to the Talent Plus Viewpoint Blog.

A graduate of the University of Nebraska–Lincoln, Kim earned a BA in English and psychology (1990), an MS in psychology (1994), and a PhD in cognitive psychology (1997). She was a Presidential Fellow in 1997. During her time as a graduate student and later as an adjunct faculty member, she taught undergraduate courses in research methods and data analysis, perception, cognition, and introductory psychology. Her professional experience also includes hands-on training, management, and strategic leadership of more than 500 volunteers as director of ministries for Southwood Lutheran Church.

In her free time, Kim enjoys coaching high school track, reading, writing, and getting outdoors around her home in Highlands Ranch, Colorado. She and her husband, Rick, have three children, Connor, Arin, and Peyton.

INDEX

Note: Page references in *italics* refer to figures.